Enjoy your garden

HOUSE PLANTS IN COLOR

Edited by
FRANCIS B. STARK & CONRAD B. LINK

DOUBLEDAY & COMPANY, INC.

Horticultural Consultants: Francis C. Stark, Professor and Chairman, Department of Horticulture, University of Maryland; Conrad B. Link, Professor of Horticulture, University of Maryland

NOTE: The horticultural consultants have checked botanical terms against Bailey, *Standard Cyclopedia of Horticulture,* and other sources, but have used as the final authority Bailey and Bailey, *Hortus Second.* Some botanical varieties named by the authors have been retained even if they appear in none of our sources.

The original edition of this book was written in Italian, primarily for Italian gardeners. We have endeavored to preserve some of the rhetorical flavor of the Italian authors, while adapting the cultural and hardiness recommendations to the United States.

Picture Credits

Fotografie: C. Mariorossi: copertina; M. Bavestrelli: 116, 119, 122, 124, 136; C. Bevilacqua: 1, 2, 3, 4, 8, 9, 10, 12, 13, 14, 15, 16, 17, 18, 19, 21, 22, 23, 24, 25, 26, 27, 28, 30, 31, 32, 33, 34, 36, 38, 39, 40, 41, 42, 43, 44, 45, 46, 47, 48, 49, 51, 52, 54, 55, 56, 57, 58, 59, 60, 61, 62, 63, 64, 65, 66, 67, 68, 73, 74, 75, 76, 77, 78, 79, 80, 83, 84, 85, 87, 88, 89, 90, 92, 93, 94, 95, 96, 97, 98, 100, 101, 102, 103, 104, 107, 109, 110, 111, 112, 114, 115, 120, 121, 127, 128, 130, 140, 143, 146, 147, 148, 149, 150, 151, 152, 153, 154, 155, 158, 159, 161, 162, 163, 164, 165, 167, 168, 169, 170, 173, 174, 175, 176, 177, 178, 181, 183, 184, 185, 186; Bravo: 117–126; Etrusko: 139; Archivio I.G.D.A.: 5, 6, 11, 20, 29, 50, 53, 69, 72, 106, 108, 123, 129, 131, 133, 141, 156, 157, 160; A. Margiocco: 113, 118; P. Martini: 37, 105, 132; G. Mazza: 7, 145, 166; M. Pedone: 81, 82, 125, 134, 135, 137, 138, 142, 144; P2: 91; P. Popper: 182; S. Prato: 86, 171, 172; F. Quilici: 70; Servizio Giardini Torino: 99, 179, 180.

© ISTITUTO GEOGRAFICO DE AGOSTINI S.p.A. – NOVARA – 1969

ISBN: 0-385-02894-6
Published under arrangement with
Ottenheimer Publishers, Inc.
Baltimore, Maryland
Manufactured in Italy by I.G.D.A.

Table of Contents

Greenhouse gardening

Plants have been associated with man from his very beginnings. He has used them not only as food but for his own personal adornment and for decoration of his surroundings. This is well documented in the ruins of ancient structures, in the uncovered city of Pompeii, and in the drawings and paintings down through the centuries. Many works of art and handicrafts of all kinds have designs which are based on plants and flowers; in some cases, the actual reproduction of the plant or flower has been detailed sufficiently to allow for precise identification.

The cultivation of plants and flowers is not only a commercial industry but one which is enjoyed throughout the world by all persons regardless of their social or financial standing. Evidence of man's horticultural involvement is provided by the single geranium plant in the window of a simple home, as well by the elaborate garden surrounding a large mansion. Gardening is the most popular of hobbies and is of interest to persons of all ages.

Plants and flowers from the garden not only beautify the surroundings, but many enliven and enhance interior decoration as well. They make our indoor environment more attractive and more livable. They add a distinctive touch to any room, to make the house a home.

Greenhouses offer to the home gardener an opportunity to grow and to work with plants throughout the year.

Greenhouses: what they are

A greenhouse is a structure covered with a material that transmits light. Traditionally the material has been glass, but in recent years, plastics of several kinds and textures have been used. These may be thin films that are useful for only a few months or rigid materials that are satisfactory for 8 to 10 or more years.

The greenhouse is an enclosed structure, and thus allows for the regulation of the environment surrounding the plant. It provides us with the opportunity to control light and temperature as well as soil quality, nutrition, and water, and hence gives us the ability to establish as specific an environment as may be necessary for the culture of any plant.

The manufacturers of greenhouses have designed many styles and sizes that can be adapted by the home greenhouse gardener to meet his particular requirements in the home landscape. The structure may be free standing or attached to the house or garage. A person who likes to build may buy one and erect it himself or he may prefer to design and construct his own.

Greenhouse classification

Greenhouses may be classified according to their length of expected use or to their degree of permanence. The conventional structure is rigidly built with a solid foundation and covered with glass or a rigid plastic of a quality to last many years. Such a structure may be constructed of wood and supported with pipe posts or a steel frame or it may be constructed entirely of aluminum supported with the metal posts. Typically the roof has a uniform slope, although older houses, the so-called display houses, may have a slightly curved roof and curved eaves. There are minor variations in the sizes and shapes of the parts of a greenhouse made by different companies.

The size of a greenhouse is adjustable and varies with the manufacturer. Essentially the length is a multiple of the width of the glass that is used on the roof. The side walls should be at least 6 feet tall so as to allow a person to stand erect.

Greenhouse shape is another method of classification. An even-span house is one with an equal slope on either side of the ridge. The section supports may be attached parallel to each other, fastening them at the ridge at the top and at the eave line. In this arrangement the construction is referred to as a ridge and furrow construction. The section supports may be separated a uniform distance from each other and attached to a connecting structure or greenhouse; in this arrangement the construction is referred to as a detached house.

A lean-to greenhouse is essentially one half of an even-span house attached in its lengthwise dimension to a building. This shape is common for a home greenhouse where it may have the advantage of using the home heating system.

Greenhouse manufacturers are now making both even-span and lean-to style greenhouses designed for a simple foundation, to be erected by the purchaser. Certain of these have large panes of glass that extend to the ground level and this allows the light to extend directly to the floor level which gives an opportunity to grow plants under the benches.

A temporary greenhouse is one usually constructed of lighter structural materials and covered with a plastic film. Such structures are used to extend the growing season either at the beginning, as a method of starting young plants in the spring, or at the end, to protect any plants from early frost in the fall. For example, commercially temporary green-houses are used in the spring to start annual plants or in the fall to prevent a crop of chrysanthemums from being injured by an early frost.

Greenhouses may be classified on the basis of the tempera-ture maintained or the type of plants to be grown. A warm temperature, 20 to 24° C (68–75° F), is used for certain types of orchids, foliage plants, desert plants, or others that need a warm night temperature. A medium temperature house of 16–20° C (60–68° F) or a cool house of 10–12° C (50–53° F) are used for plants requiring lower night temperatures. Roses, certain orchids, azaleas, poinsettias, and chrysanthe-mums prefer the medium temperature while carnations would be grown in the cool temperature.

For a home hobby greenhouse, where a great variety of plants are to be grown, the style of the structure is not impor-tant. Rather the temperature and the light conditions are most important, and these can be regulated to accommodate the greatest number of plants in the greenhouse. Fortunately, plants are tolerant of a wide range of conditions and will grow, even if everything in the environment is not to their exact requirements. They may be slower to develop or not flower as early, but they will grow.

Site for the greenhouse (orientation)

Ideally, a north-south direction for the long dimension of the greenhouse may be most desirable to obtain maximum light. Modern greenhouses, because of newer styles of con-struction and the use of larger pieces of glass, have less superstructure and thus there is less shadow from the sup-portive parts; consequently less attention is now paid to the compass orientation. Other factors do enter into the selection of a site, however. Protection provided by other buildings, by walls, a hedge, or a wooded area are all important in reducing wind and air movement. Avoid locations where tall trees or tall structures would shade the greenhouse. If the land slopes, select the slope facing south to take advantage of the greater amount of sun on the greenhouse during the winter months.

Heating the greenhouse

Heating systems for the small greenhouse have been de-signed for efficiency and ease of operation. The system of heating will be influenced by the kind of plants to be grown. Remember that even the warmest temperature needed may be only 20 to 24° C (68–75° F). This requirement is based on the temperature at night and may, in fact, be necessary for only a few kinds of orchids or foliage plants. Many kinds will grow better at a medium temperature of 16 to 18° C (60 to 65° F), and others still cooler.

It is advisable to rely on the greenhouse manufacturer's recommendations about the heating requirements, which will vary with the temperature requirements for the plants to be grown and with the climate. The number of pipes for a hot water or a steam system, and their location and placement in the house, are influenced by the temperature to be main-tained.

A hot water heating system provides steady heat and does not fluctuate suddenly. It is rather easily controlled. A steam system provides heat rapidly and is easily expanded when more greenhouses are built. If the greenhouse is attached to a house, it may be possible to connect either of these systems to the home heating system. Likewise in the case of a hot air system. Thermostats for greenhouse temperature control should be installed to separate the heat demands of the home from the greenhouse. Often the home will need heat during the daytime while the greenhouse is getting sufficient heat from the sun. During the night when the home temperatures are turned down and outdoor temperatures are lower, the greenhouse then needs the heat.

Greenhouses that are free standing will need their own heating system. This is generally located in the workroom or service building to which they are attached. The system should be of a type that will use the most economical fuel, natural gas, propane or bottled gas, or oil. All of these may be regulated with devices to simplify the daily care and atten-tion. Avoid the use of a space heater in the greenhouse since there is possible damage from gas due to leaks or improper combustion. Such heaters must be vented to the outside.

Temperature control (cooling the greenhouse)

A greenhouse is essentially a "heat trap." When the sun hits the glass, the temperature rises rapidly. Even on a cold day, below freezing, if there is little wind, the temperatures may be very high and require some ventilation. The tempera-ture requirements for a plant are always given in reference to the night temperature. Daytime temperatures are allowed to rise some 10 to 15 degrees higher before ventilation is given. During many months of the year, this means that even the night temperature is higher than may be desirable.

WOODEN-FRAME GREENHOUSE

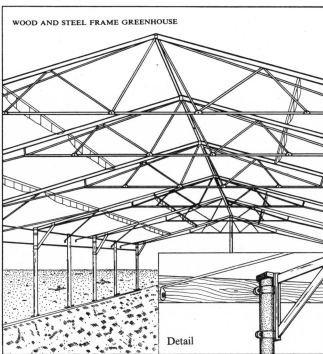

WOOD AND STEEL FRAME GREENHOUSE

Detail

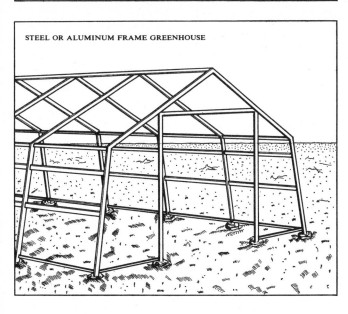

STEEL OR ALUMINUM FRAME GREENHOUSE

A greenhouse typically has ventilators installed at the ridge and often on the side wall as well. The ridge ventilators may be equipped with an electrically controlled device that is activated by a thermostat to automatically open and close the ventilators.

Exhaust fans may be installed at one end of the house with an opening at the opposite end, thermostatically operated to exhaust the air to the outside when the temperatures are high.

A common practice during the seasons of the year (late spring, summer, and early fall) when the temperatures are high and the light intensity strong, is to spray or paint the outside of the greenhouse to reduce the light intensity and thereby to help reduce the interior temperatures. Whitewash, whiting, and diluted water paints are used. Generally they will need to be brushed or scrubbed off in the fall.

Slat or lath shades, installed in a roller type of arrangement on the outside of the greenhouse, are available. Orchid houses sometimes are shaded with these, and it gives an opportunity to regulate the shading from day to day if this is desirable. Cheesecloth or light grades of muslin suspended in some convenient way may be installed inside over groups of plants.

In areas of low humidity, cooling systems which have a pad of a material such as excelsior that is kept moist installed at one side of the house and an exhaust fan on the opposite side allow the air to be drawn through the house. In this process of moving the moist air, the air inside is cooled somewhat. This is less effective in regions of a naturally high humidity than in areas where the summer air is normally fairly dry.

Construction materials and utilities

The most modern greenhouses are now using extruded aluminum for all supportive parts of the structure. In larger houses, some of the superstructure may be of steel. Aluminum is slightly more expensive than wood but, in the long run is cheaper. It is durable and does not need painting.

When steel is used for supports, either as pipe or of a structural design, it should be galvanized to reduce maintenance and assure durability.

Wood for greenhouses is generally redwood or cypress. Both are durable and when additionally protected with paint make a satisfactory material excepting for the repainting that is necessary. When painting wood, use a good quality white oil-base paint that does not contain any mercury fungicidal material. Aluminum paints are sometimes used, but they do not reflect the light as well as white paint. The heating pipes in a greenhouse are not painted.

Flat drawn glass is used for greenhouses, generally grade B of a double thickness.

Plastics are now available for covering such structures. Polyethylene and polyvinyl films are used. They are effective for 8 to 12 months, but are easily damaged by storms and heavy winds. Rigid forms of plastics are available in large panels, often large enough to extend from the ridge to the eave without a joint, making a leakproof roof.

A greenhouse should be provided with water and electricity. Water is generally available from the same source as that which supplies the house. Faucets should be located in one or more places to attach a hose for watering. Automatic watering systems are possible for a home greenhouse and, once they have been installed, reduce the daily care. Water should also be available to use in a mist system.

While an electrical source is not essential for a greenhouse, it becomes necessary if automatic controls for heating or a mist system are used, and for circulating fans, and the use of additional lights. Supplementary lighting is necessary if certain plants are to be grown out of season and in those cases where long days are necessary for flower formation and development.

The workroom

A service area is necessary to operate a small greenhouse and this is generally in a workroom attached to it or if the greenhouse is attached to the house or garage then work space should be provided close at hand. The workroom would include space for the heating system if there is need for a separate system.

The workroom should include a work table and cupboards or shelves for storing supplies, for tools and equipment, and for such items as pots, pesticides, extra soil, and organic materials. Pesticides should be stored in a place that can be locked.

The exterior of the workroom should be of a style or design to fit in with other buildings.

Other structures

In addition to the conventional greenhouse, glass- or plastic-covered frames may provide additional growing space for propagation, for starting young plants, or for storage of certain plants over the winter. If heat is supplied to such a frame, it is referred to as a hot bed; otherwise they are called cold frames.

Soils

In selecting a soil for the growing of plants in the greenhouse, choose one with a good texture, loose and crumb-like. Soils that have had sod growing on them for at least a year or more generally have a good structure. If the soil is a loam,

so much the better. Clay soils are usable if they have a good structure although they are likely to loose it rather quickly. Sandy soils have a loose texture. Fertility can be added to the soil later but the soil structure cannot be changed.

Modern greenhouse practices are developing more toward the use of soil mixtures. Generally this is a combination of a soil plus organic matter and perhaps including some inert material.

A composted soil is essentially a mixture, made in advance, by building a pile of alternate layers of soil and organic materials. This organic matter may be leaves, garden refuse, straw, animal manures, or any inexpensive organic material. After such a pile has been constructed for 6 to 8 months, it is ready to use. Cut the pile down in such a manner that the soil and organic matter are mixed. To speed up the process of rotting, the pile may be cut down and rebuilt before using. Fertilizers such as superphosphate and even some nitrogen forms may be included as the pile is built. A compost pile would be a way in which the home gardener could reuse soil from old plants.

Soil mixtures are made as needed. These are mixtures of a soil, an organic matter such as peat, and, if a very loose final product is needed, sand, perlite or vermiculite may be included. The proportion of each can be varied, but a mixture of equal parts by volume of each is practical.

Organic matter for greenhouse soils is usually peat. Decomposed leaves may be available and depending on location other things may be available such as decomposed animal manures, straw, various grasses, and others. Peat is convenient for the home gardener because it is essentially sterile and free of weed seed and is easy to handle.

Soils or soil mixtures for most plants should be slightly acid. If the soil or the soil mixture has a soil reaction with a pH of 6.0 or lower, then lime should be added during preparation. Only a few plants, such as azaleas, rhododendrons, gardenia, and *Erica* will want an acid soil.

Certain orchids, especially the epiphytic kinds, are not grown in soil but in osmunda fiber, which is the fibrous roots and stem of the Osmunda fern, or in shredded redwood or fir bark. The terrestial types are grown in soil mixtures usually having a very high percentage of organic matter and often using sphagnum moss and a shreded bark.

Several commercially-prepared soil mixtures are being sold for greenhouse use. They are primarily a mixture of peat and perlite or vermiculite, thoroughly mixed and of a uniform grade. These are packaged in conveniently sized bags and may also be used for starting seed and for vegetative propagation, as well as for general potting.

Fertilizers

Nitrogen, phosphorus, and potassium are the three nutrient elements that are most commonly lacking in soil and that are added as fertilizers. Such materials may be added in a dry form as the soil is prepared or in a liquid form after the plant has been planted. The liquid types are water soluble and may be applied in very dilute concentrations every time the plant is watered or in a more concentrated form less frequently. The inorganic fertilizers, in either the dry or liquid form, may supply only one element or, in certain cases, two elements. Commercial mixtures generally supply the three nutrient elements named and often include one or more of the so-called minor elements such as iron, boron, or manganese which, in very minute quantities, are necessary for plant growth.

The inorganic fertilizers are the least expensive to use, when based on the amount of nutrients they supply. Organic fertilizers are not available to the plant until they have been decomposed.

Inorganic fertilizer sources are those manufactured especially or that are by-products of certain manufacturing processes. These include ammonium sulfate, calcium sulfate, sodium nitrate, ammonium nitrate, and urea that supply nitrogen; superphosphate which supplies phosphorus; and potassium chloride or potassium sulfate that supply potassium.

The inorganic fertilizers have their origin primarily from certain animals, as a by-product. Organic nitrogen sources include horn and hoof shavings, dried blood, and fish meal; phosphorus may be supplied from bonemeal; and wood ashes are an organic source of potassium. Organic fertilizers may vary slightly from time to time in the exact amount of fertilizer element they supply, and may actually contribute traces of some other elements when decomposing. This is influenced by the treatment that is followed in processing for fertilizer use.

Lime is not considered to be a fertilizer; rather its greatest effect is to make the soil less acid and to help improve soil structure. Calcium does become available to the plant from the lime incorporated in the soil.

Animal manures are not commonly available and are variable as to their fertility value which is influenced by the kind of animal, its diet, the amount of bedding material included, and the care of the manure before application to the soil. The greatest value of manure is not as a fertilizer, but rather as a source of organic matter which has a beneficial influence on improving soil structure.

In a well-constructed greenhouse with a tight roof, there is little air change if the ventilators are closed. Under winter conditions, with a heavy mass of plant growth in the house, a bright sun, and actively growing plants, it is possible that the carbon dioxide content of the air in the greenhouse may become insufficient for good plant growth. It has been found that growth is increased by injecting carbon dioxide into the atmosphere. This is done commercially under selected conditions. For a home greenhouse, this practice is probably not necessary. The addition of carbon dioxide has been referred to as "aerial fertilization."

For the home greenhouse operator, it will be most convenient to use commercially-prepared fertilizers, which are usually mixtures of materials that supply nitrogen, phosphorus, and potassium and are referred to as a "complete fertilizer." Such kinds are available both in a dry form to be mixed into the soil in advance of planting or as a top dressing, or are made of water soluble materials that can be dissolved in water and applied to the soil in liquid form.

A newer fertilizer type is the slow-release or slow-acting kind that may be mixed into the soil and remain effective for many months. One form is a soluble material "encapsulated" in a plastic-like material which, when in contact with the soil moisture, gradually releases the fertilizer to the soil solution and is then made available to the plant.

Propagation

Propagation of plants is possible by two methods:
1. By the seed—the sexual method.
2. By vegetative means—the asexual methods. There are many forms of this and the form to use varies with different plants. For some plants only one method is effective while, for other plants, several methods may be used.

Seed propagation

Seed is the method generally used for propagation of the species and for any plant that will come "true-to-type" by this method; that is, where the seedling will produce a plant similar to the plant from which it came. Seed is used in breeding programs where plants of different genetic make-ups are crossed in order to obtain new kinds.

Some seeds are sown in the area where they are to grow. Plants that do not transplant easily are handled in this way, sown in place. Among our ornamental plants, this is necessary for only a few kinds of annuals. Most seed is sown in a medium that is loose, porous, well aerated and yet will hold water. Such a medium can be prepared by mixing soil with organic matter and perhaps some inert material. In outdoor beds, this may be accomplished by merely selecting a suitable spot with well-drained soil. Mixtures of materials include peat and perlite, or peat and vermiculite, or perhaps other mixtures that might include soil, sand, or similar inert substances.

Seed may be sown in beds out of doors or in the home at a window, in a greenhouse, or in protective frames such as a cold frame or hot bed. Seed should be scattered over the seed bed uniformly and then be lightly covered. Tiny seeds such as those of begonia, calceolaria, petunia, or azalea are not covered, but are merely pressed into the soil. For seed of these kinds, covering the soil with a thin layer of finely-screened sphagnum makes a good material for the seed.

When the seed has germinated, thin out the weak seedlings and those that are crowded to allow those remaining to have greater space for development. When the seedlings have developed their first true leaf, they are ready for transplanting. Transplant them to seed beds, spacing them to allow for development, and then later transplant them again to where they are to grow. Or they may be transplanted to pots, flats or other containers. Rapidly-growing kinds are often transplanted from the seed bed to the place where they are to grow to full development.

Vegetative propagation

Since plants produced from seed may not come true-to-type or may require too long a period of time before coming into flower or developing mature characteristics, a vegetative method is often selected. Plants vary in the part of the plant

Layering is a form of propagation where a branch is bent down to the soil and covered, leaving the tip exposed. Often a wound is made in the stem portion that is covered. After roots develop, the branch is cut at the end nearest the parent and the new plant is replanted. Air layering is a method often used on foliage plants that have become too tall. A wound is made in the stem, a bit of wood is placed in the wound to hold it open, and the wound is dusted with a root-promoting hormone. The entire area is covered with moist sphagnum moss and wrapped with plastic or aluminium foil. The moss must be kept moist. After roots have developed into the moss, the stem is severed below this area and the tip with develop-

Preparation of a leaf cutting. On the left, make small incisions through the veins on the underside of the leaf. On the right, the leaf is stretched out and made fast to the soil with hairpins. In the lower figure, the adventitious roots are seen developing.

Propagation by division of a plant.

that may be used for propagation; depending on the kind of plant, it may be the stem, leaves, or the roots. In some plants, vegetative methods merely use the parts of the plant that naturally account for the increase, such as the bulbs, tubers, rhizomes, stolons, or off-shoot runners. Propagation may also be achieved by dividing of the plant which involves its separation into smaller parts, by layering, or by grafting or budding.

Tubers, bulbs, rhizomes, and runners are essentially modified stems which can produce new roots when separated from the mother plant. Once removed, they often already can be immediately replanted.

ing roots is potted as a new plant. The technique of air layering can be used in the case of a few woody plants outdoors.

Cuttings are perhaps the most common method of vegetative propagation. Cuttings are made from strong, healthy stems. The tip is used, generally with 3 to 4 nodes, varying with the kind of plant, and often similar sections of the lower portions of the stem can be selected as well. The season of propagation varies with the plant. Soft immature growth is not satisfactory, rather it should be fully developed, although the growth may not need to be fully mature. Such growth is referred to as a soft-wood cutting or as a greenwood or herbaceous cutting. Other cuttings may be semi-woody or fully developed and woody. Cuttings are propagated in sand, peat, perlite or vermiculite, or perhaps some other inert, pest-free material. Some gardeners will make a mixture of these kinds. Loose porous soil is also used especially when propagating outdoors.

In the greenhouse, propagation is done in a shaded location, either by shading the plants or the glass above. The humidity should be high. The use of a misting system to keep the cuttings moist is excellent. This can be made automatic, thus reducing the care and attention. During the fall, winter, and spring months, the rooting of many cuttings is hastened

These preparations are available in small sized packages for the home greenhouse operator. They contain chemicals such as indole-acetic acid, indole-butyric acid, or salts of these acids with other related chemicals.

The leaves from certain types of plants may be used for propagation. Mature leaves are removed from a plant such as *Saintpaulia* and inserted into a propagating medium in the same manner as a stem cutting. A new plant will develop at the base and when it is large enough to handle conveniently, it is potted as a new plant. Leaves of peperomia may be handled in the same way. Leaves of certain begonias, especially *Begonia Rex,* are laid on a moist propagation medium

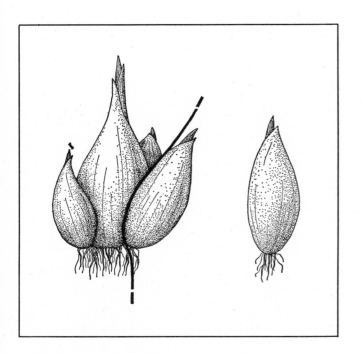

Division of bulblets surrounding a mature bulb.

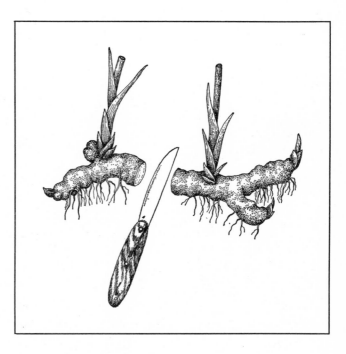

Propagation by division of a rhizome.

if the medium is several degrees warmer than the air temperature. Heating pipes located below the propagation bench or the use of an electric heating cable are ways in which this can be accomplished and be controlled.

Root-promoting chemicals speed up the time of rooting and ensure that a higher percentage of cuttings will root. Commercial preparations of these are available in either a dry or liquid form. The dry form is a powder, and the stem end is dipped into it before it is placed in the propagation medium. The liquid kinds are either ready to use or need to be diluted with water. In either case, the stem end is dipped into or soaked in the solution before being put in the medium.

and new plants will develop at the base as well as at any wound that is made in the large leaf veins (see the illustration on the left-hand side of p. 8.). Leaves of the *Sansevieria* may be cut into sections 2 to 3 inches long and treated in the same way.

Division is a simple method of propagation. Division is used and is demonstrated in the illustrations above and on page 10 for those plants that form a cluster of many stems. The plant is removed from the pot and the stems or crowns are cut apart into smaller pieces. Usually this is done when the plant is in its least active period of growth. The practice is the same as that used for perennial plants outdoors.

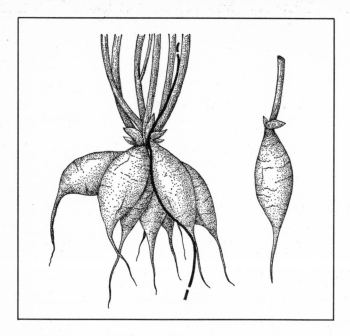

Propagation by division of a tuberous root.

Grafting and the related technique of budding are seldom used for greenhouse plants. An appropriate understock is selected and a scion of the desired plant is attached or the bud inserted. The methods of taking care of the grafted or budded plants and the season of the year in which it is done vary with the kind of plant. Fruit trees, some azaleas, roses, and lilacs are familiar plants that are grafted. Cactus are sometimes grafted, to produce odd-shaped plants; an example is the practice of grafting the Christmas Cactus, *Schlumbergera* or *Zygocactus,* onto *Pereskia* to form a tree-like plant.

Pests

Plants in the greenhouse are subjected to pests just as they are out of doors. In some respects it is easier to control the pests in a greenhouse since there is a rapid plant growth. The foliage may be kept dry which may be important in the spread of disease, and having the plants enclosed gives and opportunity to fumigate or use an aerosol pesticide.

There are several major groups of greenhouse pests, insects, diseases, physiological disorders, and other animal pests.

Plants which suffer from physiological problems often appear as if they had been affected by an insect or a disease. Leaf damage or irregularities may be caused by a mineral deficiency or excess, expecially of the three major elements most commonly lacking from soils (nitrogen, phosphorus, and potassium) and on occasion, other elements such as magnesium or boron. A lack of each element produces a distinctive reaction in the plant yet the deficiency is sometimes difficult to diagnose since some diseases may also show similar symptoms. Toxic substances in the atmosphere may cause marginal injury to leaves or interfere with normal leaf development.

Improper conditions in the environment such as excess or insufficient light for a given plant may cause unnatural growth, such as foliage that is excessively large or small or an unnatural leaf color for that plant. Constant excess or insufficient water in the soil will influence plant growth and eventually the size, and perhaps flower formation as well. Soil problems are corrected by the proper fertilizer applications while excess applications can be leached from the soil by frequent, heavy watering provided the soil has good drainage.

Oedemia, the development of swellings or outgrowths on the lower side of the leaf of certain plants is associated with an excessive supply of water in the soil and high humidity in the greenhouse. It is peculiarly a greenhouse problem.

The more typical diseases include the virus diseases and those caused by bacteria or by fungi.

Virus diseases are caused by a submicroscopic organism that spreads rapidly through the infected plant. It is spread by contact from an affected plant to a healthy one. It is found in the vascular system and generally there is no control for it. Some virus diseases develop so rapidly that the plant is dwarfed and shows characteristic leaf patterns of green and yellow. A few virus diseases seem not to do much damage and may be present without injury. This is true for some variegated plants, where the variegation is actually caused by a virus. Most virus diseases are rather specific for a given plant while others may infect many kinds. There are no effective controls for virus, rather use care in selecting propagating material and rogue out infected plants.

Bacterial diseases develop when becteria enter the plant through a wound and cause their damage. Most rot or decaying diseases are caused by bacteria as well as certain leaf spots, leaf blights, and galls.

Fungi cause other types of injury, again they may appear as a leaf spot, or leaf blight, as cankers on a stem, as mildew or as rust on a leaf or stem. Diseases that cause the plant to wilt are also caused by a fungus.

Damping off, the dying of seedlings and young plants by rotting at the soil line or just below, may be caused by several disease organisms. Soil sterilization and seed or soil treatment with a fungicide are effective controls, actually precautions for the prevention of this problem.

For the control of disease in a greenhouse, first be certain that the soil and environment are correct for the plant, then remove infected parts if possible and use a recommended fungicide, following the directions. Disease controls are constantly changing but currently recommended fugicides include ferbam, captan, and zinc-, sulfer-, copper-containing materials.

Insect pests include many of the same kinds found outdoors. These include aphids, thrips, scale insects, leaf chewing kinds, white fly, and spider mites. Insects may attack many kinds of plants in great contrast to certain diseases that may be found on only one species or closely-related species.

Aphids typically are found on rapidly-growing tips of plants and injure the plant by sucking the juices. Thrips are very tiny and feed on the underside of the leaf, sucking the juices and causing a silvery appearance on the surface. Scale insects are sucking insects that attach themselves to stems and leaves and are covered with a waxy or shell-like covering which makes them more difficult to control. Mealy bugs are soft white insects, "mealy" in appearance, found in the axils of the leaves and at the tip, and cause damage by sucking the plant sap. Control is difficult because of this waxy covering. Cyclamen mites attack the growing shoots of the African violet, cyclamen, begonia, gloxinia and other gesneriads, causing the new growth to be stunted or deformed, and preventing the plant from developing properly. White Fly is a small white insect from the tropics and can become difficult to control. The adults are moth like, covered with a white waxy powder and fly about when the plant is disturbed. This insect lays its eggs on the underside of the leaves of many greenhouse plants; the immature stages are a pale greenish color, semitransparent and cause damage by sucking the plant juices. Lantana, cineraria, fuchsia, ageratum, tomatoes, and poinsettias are favorites of this insect.

The control of insects involves using a spray or dust. The recommended materials are being altered so rapidly to conform to acceptable safety standards that commercial preparations should be selected for control. Many insects are most easily controlled when they are in their immature stages, and the plant should be thoroughly covered with the material, both on the top and the lower side of the leaf. It is a good greenhouse practice to inspect all plants before they are brought into the greenhouse for pests and to spray them first. Sometimes a thorough washing of the foliage with warm soapy water will dislodge the pests and this is then followed by clear water to remove the suds. Syringing of the plants with water under a spray-like force will dislodge many insects and if it is done routinely, may give control, especially during seasons when insects cannot come in from outdoors.

There is still another group of insect-related pests, not true insects, but for practical purposes often considered with them that will cause damage. These include sowbugs or pillbugs, an oval-shaped pest with many legs, that curl into a ball when disturbed. Millipedes also have many legs, are typically dark shiny brown and move rapidly. These two pests are common under flats, pots, and in dark areas where they feed on decaying organic matter, and are usually harmless to growing plants. However, they may attack seedlings and young plants when they become numerous. Slugs or slimy snails without a shell and snails with a shell may be a greenhouse nuisance beacause they feed not only on decaying matter but on seedlings or on soft succulent leaves and new growth. Control for these is by baits, as metaldehyde or beer.

Nematodes are still another soil pest that may attack the root and some forms attack the leaves. These are also called eel worms; they penetrate the tissue and in the case of roots may cause a swelling or an enlargement. Foliage nematodes effect damage by causing spots or sections of a leaf to turn brown, as on begonia or the chrysanthemum. For soil nematodes, soil sterilization is the best control; the planting of pest-free material is also advantageous. Foliar types are controlled by sprays.

Glossary

*1. **Achene**—a dry, hard, indehiscent, single-seeded fruit with a single carpel.

2. **Acaulescent**—stemless

3. **Acuminate**—tapering to a point.

4. **Adnate**—united, grown together.

5. **Adventitious**—originating at other than the usual place; *roots* originating from any structure other than a root; *buds* arising from a part of the plant other than terminal or node.

6. **Alternate** (leaves)—one leaf at each node but alternating in direction.

7. **Annual**—a plant with a one-year life cycle.

8. **Anther**—that part of the stamen containing the pollen.

9. **Apetalous**—lacking petals.

10. **Apical**—terminal or summit.

11. **Axil**—the angle between a leaf and stem.

*12. **Berry**—a simple, fleshy fruit developed from a single ovule (loosely, any pulpy or juicy fruit).

13. **Biennial**—a plant with a two-year life cycle.

14. **Blade**—the expanded part of a leaf or leaflet.

*15. **Blossom**—the flower of a seed plant.

16. **Bract**—a specialized, modified leaf; of leaf-like structure.

17. **Bud**—a compressed stem; an underdeveloped stem.

18. **Bulb**—underground storage and reproductive organ with fleshy leaves called bulb scales.

19. **Calyx**—the outermost of the floral parts, composed of sepals.

*20. **Campanulate**—bell-shaped.

21. **Capitate**—shaped like a head.

*22. **Capsule**—a dry, dehiscent, multi-seeded fruit of more than one carpel.

23. **Carpel**—a leaf-like structure bearing ovules along the margins; a simple pistil.

*24. **Cauline**—related to an obvious stem or axis.

25. **Comose**—having tufts of hair.

*26. **Cordate**—heart-shaped.

27. **Corm**—an enlarged, underground stem, serving as a storage organ for food reserves.

28. **Corolla**—an inner cycle of floral organs, comprising the petals.

29. **Corymb**—a flat-topped, indeterminate flower cluster, with pedicels originating along a central peduncle; outer flowers open first.

30. **Cotyledons**—the first (seed) leaves of the embryo.

31. **Crenate**—toothed with rounded teeth.

32. **Crispate**—curled.

33. **Culm**—the stem of a grass or sedge.

34. **Cultivar**—a variety developed from known hybridization or origin.

35. **Cuneate**—triangular, wedge-shaped.

36. **Cyme**—a determinate flower cluster in which the central flower opens first.

37. **Deciduous**—plants that drop their leaves at the end of each season.

38. **Dehiscent**—opening of an anther or a fruit, permitting escape of pollen or seeds.

39. **Dentate**—toothed along the margins, apex sharp.

40. **Dichotomous**—divided into pairs; forked branches roughly equal.

41. **Dicotyledonous**—having two cotyledons.

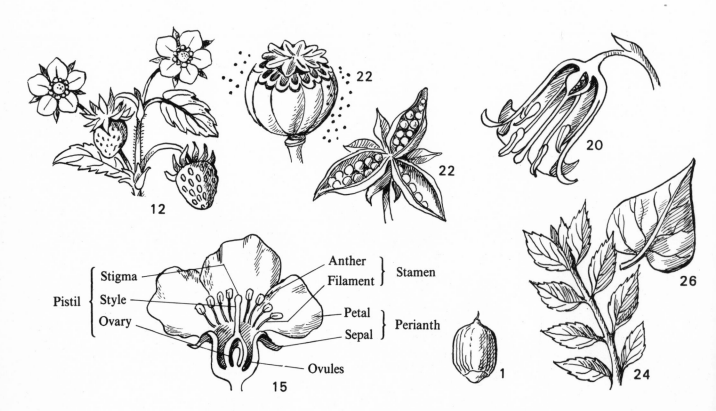

42. **Digitate** (leaves)—with leaflets arising from the apex of the petiole.

43. **Dioecious**—a species having male and female flowers on different, individual plants.

44. **Distichous**—in two vertical ranks, as the leaves of grasses.

*45. **Drupe**—a simple fleshy fruit, single carpel, with a hard endocarp containing the seed, e.g., the peach.

46. **Embryo**—a rudimentary plant.

47. **Entire**—without dentation or division.

48. **Epiphyte**—a plant that grows on another but is not parasitic.

49. **Fasciated**—an abnormally wide and flat stem.

50. **Filament**—the part of the stamen supporting the anther.

51. **Follicle**—a dry, dehiscent fruit with a single carpel, which dehisces along the ventral suture.

52. **Frond**—the leaf of a fern.

53. **Glabrous**—without hairs or pubescence.

54. **Glaucous**—covered with a whitish "bloom."

55. **Habit**—the general appearance of a plant.

*56. **Head**—a short, dense inflorescence, frequently with ray flowers around the margins and *tubular* disk flowers inside.

57. **Herbaceous**—non-woody.

58. **Hirsute**—hairy.

59. **Humus**—incompletely decomposed organic materials in the soil.

60. **Hybrid**—the result of a cross between two parents differing in genetic composition.

61. **Hydrophyte**—water loving; a plant adapted to wet conditions; capable of growing in water.

62. **Imbricate**—overlapping vertically or spirally.

63. **Indehiscent**—fruits remaining closed at maturity.

64. **Inflorescence**—the arrangement of flowers in a cluster; a complete flower cluster.

65. **Internode**—the part of a stem between two nodes.

66. **Involucre**—a cycle of bracts subtending a flower or an inflorescence.

67. **Keel**—the two front, united petals of most leguminous flowers, e.g., pea.

*68. **Lanceolate**—lance-shaped, narrow and tapered at the ends, widening above the base and narrowed to the apex.

*69. **Legume**—dry, dehiscent fruit, single carpel, usually opening along both sutures.

70. **Lenticils**—small, corky areas on woody stems.

71. **Lenticular**—lens-shaped.

72. **Ligulate**—strap-shaped.

73. **Ligule**—a thin membrane at the top of the leaf sheath in the grasses.

74. **Lip**—one portion of an unequally divided corolla; often of different sizes or colors as in orchids.

75. **Monoecious**—having male and female flowers on the same plant.

76. **Morphology**—form, structure, and development.

77. **Needle**—the long, narrow leaf characteristic of the conifers, as pine and spruce.

78. **Node**—point on a stem from which a leaf or branch emerges.

*79. **Opposite** (leaves)—two leaves at each node, opposite each other.

*80. **Palmate**—palm-like, radiating outward from the base.

*81. **Panicle**—a compound raceme.

*82. **Papilionaceous** (corolla)—a pea-like flower, having a standard keel and wings.

83. **Pedicel**—the stem of a single flower.

84. **Peduncle**—the stem of an inflorescence.

85. **Perrenial**—a plant that lives from year to year and does not die after fruiting.

86. **Perfect** (flower)—having both stamens and carpels in the same flower.

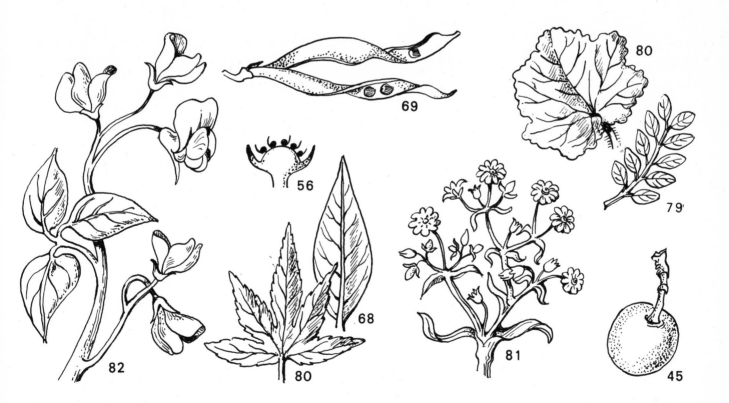

14

87. **Perianth**—the calyx and corolla.

88. **Persistent**—remaining attached.

89. **Petal**—one member of the corolla.

90. **Petiole**—the supporting stalk of the leaf blade.

91. **Pinnate**—separate leaflets arranged along a leaf stalk.

92. **Pistil**—the female reproductive parts of a flower, comprised of the stigma, style, and ovary.

*93. **Pome**—a fleshy, indehiscent fruit, with a leathery endocarp surrounding the seed, e.g., the apple.

94. **Pseudobulb**—thickened bulblike structure on leaves of epiphytic orchids.

95. **Pubescent**—covered with short hairs; downy.

96. **Raceme**—an elongated, indeterminate flower cluster with each floret on a pedicel.

97. **Rachis**—the axis of a spike.

98. **Receptacle**—the axis of a flower stalk bearing the floral parts.

99. **Reniform**—kidney-shaped.

100. **Reticulate**—as in a network of veins in a leaf.

101. **Rhizome**—an underground stem, usually horizontal, from which shoots and roots may develop.

102. **Rosette**—a cluster of leaves crowded on very short internodes.

103. **Rugose**—wrinkled.

104. **Sagittate**—arrow-shaped.

*105. **Samara**—a dry, indehiscent fruit having a wing, e.g., maple.

*106. **Scape**—a leafless flower stem arising from the soil.

107. **Schizocarp**—a dry, dehiscent fruit in which the carpels separate at maturation.

108. **Sepal**—a single member of the calyx.

109. **Septum**—a partition within an organ.

*110. **Serrate**—with sharp teeth and directed forward.

111. **Sessile**—without a stalk.

112. **Silique**—a dry, dehiscent fruit with two carpels separated by a septum.

113. **Sori**—spore masses on a fern.

*114. **Spadix**—a spike with a thick, fleshy axis, usually enveloped by a spathe.

*115. **Spathe**—a large bract or bracts surrounding an inflorescence.

116. **Spatulate**—spade-shaped; oblong with the basal end narrow.

*117. **Spike**—an inflorescence like a raceme except the florets are sessile to the peduncle.

118. **Stamen**—the male organ that bears the pollen.

119. **Standard** (in a papilionaceous corolla)—the large upper petal.

120. **Stigma**—the receptive part of the female organ.

121. **Stipule**—an appendage at the base of the petiole in some species.

122. **Stolon**—a prostrate stem that tends to root; sometimes called a runner.

123. **Style**—that part of the pistil connecting the stigma and the ovary.

124. **Succulent**—fleshy and juicy.

125. **Terrestrial**—plants growing in soil.

126. **Tomentose**—densely covered with hairs; woolly.

127. **Tuber**—underground storage organ; a stem with buds, e.g., the potato.

*128. **Umbel**—an indeterminate inflorescence in which the pedicels originate at about the same point on the peduncle and are about the same length, e.g., flowers of carrot.

*129. **Undulate**—a wavy surface.

130. **Variety**—a subdivision of a species, naturally occurring.

131. **Whorled**—leaves arranged in a circle around the stem.

132. **Wings**—(in a papilionaceous corolla)—the two side petals.

133. **Xerophyte**—a plant adapted to dry, arid conditions.

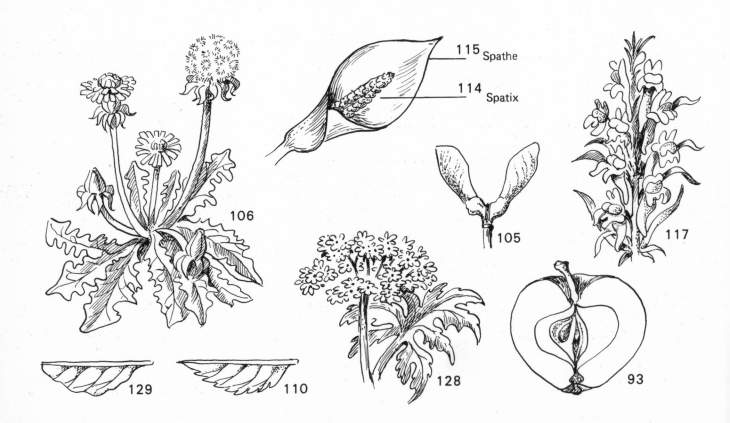

115 Spathe
114 Spatix
106
105
117
129
110
128
93

Index of plants mentioned

Pteridophytes: selaginellas, ferns

Selaginellas

Selaginellas are very small plants that can easily pass unobserved but, instead, deserve a closer look because of the elegance of their foliage.

Origins. The genus *Selaginella* belongs to the Selaginellaceae family and has about 700 species distributed throughout the tropics. Some of them can be found on walls and on rocks, or in scanty Alpine pastures, or even in sunny locations *(S. denticulata).* The species are of tropical or subtropical origin and are cultivated for ornamental purposes because of their delicate foliage.

Morphology. They are creeping or erect plants and many of them are moss-like in appearance. The leaves have a spiral arrangement in erect stems, or 3 or 4 rows on prostrate stems. Their size can vary.

Their cultivation demands the shelter of an enclosed case or a greenhouse that can be cool, temperate, or warm according to the species. They require a loose and rather acid soil with much organic matter, a humid atmosphere, and diffused light. They are propagated by division.

Species and varieties. Among the species of particular ornamental value are:

1

Selaginella Martensi comes from Mexico and is among the most widely used species in cultivation with many varieties. It has little tile-shaped leaves, that are bright green and are carried by an erect stem which emerges from a creeping stolon. It is a species for cool temperatures.

S. uncinata requires a warm temperature and is native to China. It has stems that reach 25 inches and green-bluish leaves.

S. canaliculata is from the Himalayan Mountains and it is also a warm temperature species. It has bright green branches that may reach 4 feet.

S. Wildenovii is best at cool temperatures and is native to India and the East Indies. It can have stems as long as 20 feet and is vine-like.

S. caulescens, from Japan, is an type upright to a maximum of 12 inches. It is particularly fine in the *argentea* (silver), *amoena,* and *Japonica* varieties.

S. lepidophylla is native to Texas and south to Mexico and Central America. It is a "resurrection" plant, that during periods of drought bends its external branches to form a ball easily carried by the wind; when the humidity increases, the branches stretch out again and the plant starts to grow.

1. *Selaginella Kraussiana.*

2. Close view of *Selaginella Kraussiana.*

3. *Selanginella apoda*

4

Maidenhair fern

In the semi-tropics or tropics, under condi tions of high humidity and diffused light, it common to find the maidenhair fern *(Adiantu Capillus-Veneris)*. This plant has been know since antiquity and has been described by fa mous naturalists like Dioscoris, Pliny, and Theo phrastus for exaggerated therapeutic virtue

Morphology. The numerous species Adiantum (about 200), a genus of ferns of th Polypodiaceae family, come generally fro tropical zones of South America.

They are plants with an elongated rhizom which is covered with dark bracts; the fronds a always delicate and elegant, and can be bipartit bipinnate, or flagellate. The simple or palma leaves are almost always glabrous and dar green, tender or greenish blue, or yellowish.

Species and varieties. Many species Adiantum are cultivated because of their orna mental appearance; they are largely used fo floral arrangements because of the elegance an delicacy of their foliage.

With the exception of the American Maiden hair *(S. pedatum),* the *Adiantums* must be kep in a cold frame during winter. During the grow ing period, they prefer half shade with a mil temperature and abundant humidity. The so must be of a loose texture and suited to hol water. Use a mixture of leaf mold, peat, an loam soil.

They propagate naturally by spores in a hu mid environment, but are also easily propagate by division of the clumps.

The most widely spread species are: A. Cap lus-Veneris; A. tenerum var. farleyense, wit elegant forms; A. rhodophyllum and A. rube lum, that have reddish leaves when young; A birkenneadii with triangular leaves; A. cune tum, light yellow-green colored and with ve delicate branches; A. trapeziforme; A. peruvi num; and others.

6

7

8

4. Maidenhair of the *Adiantum tenerum* var. *roseu* species.

5. The common Maidenhair fern: *Adiantum Capillu Veneris.*

6. The delicate foliage of the *Adiantum tenerum* va *roseum* seen from above.

7. Close up of *Adiantum Capillus-Veneris.*

8. Close up of *Adiantum tenerum* var. *roseum.*

Pteris and nephrolepsis

These are two genera of ferns belonging to the Polypodiaceae family that have long been known and are easily cultivated as house plants. They are tropical and subtropical in origin.

Pteris. The *Pteris* genus has fronds that are attractive, leathery, glabrous or hairy, regular or irregular, pinnate or pluripinnate. Known species number about 250, but only about 30 are cultivated for ornamental purposes.

They need a light, textured soil composed of mixtures of top soils, peat, leaf mold, and sand. They propagate by spores, but division of clumps is much simpler. They are grown in a temperate or warm greenhouse.

P. biaurita, of tropical origin, is very well known in the silver *(argentea)* and *tricolor* varieties for the elegant coloration of the foliage.

P. cretica is a species for cooler temperatures that is widely grown; varieties include *crispata, sempervirens,* and *albolineata.*

P. dentata, of tropical origin, has leaves as long as 3 feet while those of *P.tremula* may be even longer.

Nephrolepsis. The *Nephrolepis* genus, also of the Polypodiaceae family, has about 30 species of tropical origin that are considered among the best ferns for house plants because of their elegance and their easy culture.

They have a short stolon-like stem covered with brown, thin fringed scales. The fronds bear pinnate leaves as long as 3 feet.

Reproduction takes place by spores, but it is easiest to divide the plant.

Among the best-known species are:

N. cordifolia, native to Japan and New Zealand. It is a species suited to cool temperatures and is cultivated in numerous forms as *Compacta, modulata,* and *pluma.*

N.acuminata with the varieties *furcans,* and *multicaps.*

N. Duffii, native to New Zealand and South Sea islands, is small sized but very pretty.

Other important species: *N. exalta. N. pectinata. N. biserrata.*

9. Ferns are much appreciated for attractive foliage: *Polypodium glaucophyllum.*

10. A specimen plant of *Nephrolepsis exaltata* var. *bostoniensis,* Boston Fern.

11. Close up of *Pteris ensiformis* var. *vistoriae.*

12. Close up of *Pteris cretica* var. *cristata.*

Asplenium

This genus of ferns belongs to the Polypodiaceae family. They have long been cultivated and Spleenwort is a common name referring to an old medicinal use.

The genus has many species (450 according to some authors, 750 according to others), found from the tropics to the mountains of Europe.

Morphology. They vary from small plants a few inches tall to large ones with leaves over 3 feet long, terrestrial, or a few tropical epiphytic species.

The rhizome is creeping or erect, covered with dark bracts. The various-shaped branches have whole or pinnate leaves, more or less erect or decumbent. Many species are cultivated as house plants or in greenhouses.

Cultivation. They require loose soil with a good supply of organic matter. They need humid atmosphere, diffused light, and a moderate temperature.

Propagation is by division of the clumps or from spores. The procumbent species and varieties are cultivated in hanging pots.

Species and varieties. The most popular species are:

A. Nidus-Avis (Bird's Nest Fern), with a whole, large and waved foliage, light-green in color, and so named because the center appears similar to a bird's nest.

A. caudatum has leaves 12 to 18 inches long.

A. Belangeri has elegantly pinnate leaves.

A. bulbiferum and *A. viviparum* have bulblets on the leaf by which they propagate.

A. radicans has a shrubby appearance.

A. sandersoni and *A. seelosii* are small.

Among our native species, both in Europe and America, with ornamental value are: *A. Ruta muraria,* a small fern of rocks and of old walls and *A. trichomanes,* sometimes called Maidenhair Spleenwort.

13. A greenhouse with ferns: in the center, on the right, a beautiful sample of *Asplenium Nidus Avis* (Bird's Nest Fern).

atycerium

The *Platyceriums* are weird and charming king and very decorative. Their name, of eek origin, means "flat horns" and it well tifies their shape.

igins. Almost all are native to the Far st (Australia, Malacca, Thailand) and some cies are native to Western Africa and Peru.

orphology. In their original habitat, the *tyceriums* live as an epiphyte on trees getting necessary nutrients by means of particular rile leaves tightly inserted on a short rhizome t adheres to the trunk with many roots. The fertile leaves are flattened and dichoto-mously divided, with an entire margin grayish-green, often pubescent. The sporancia are on the underside along the tips and margins.

Cultivation. The *Platyceriums* are species suited for hothouses and grow well in a mixture of well decomposed soil, sphagnum, and peat, in baskets, or even better, in old tree-trunks hang-ing from the walls. They need reduced light and uniform humidity. Propagation takes place by spores, which can be sown in pots in a very light soil. They can also easily be multiplied by the young little plants that develop from root buds.

They do not need any special care and live for a long time. If they are taken inside houses, it is necessary to place them in the right light and to provide the necessary humidity.

Species and varieties. The most fa-mous and most decorative species to be consid-ered is *P. bifurcatum*, commonly called "Stag horn fern" because of the characteristic resem-blance. Also cultivated is *P. wilhelmina,* and *P. grande, P. Wallchii, P. Hillii, P. angolense* and *P. coronarium.*

14. *Platycerium bifurcatum* on an old piece of cork.

15. Close up of *P. bifurcatum* with spore bearing leaf.

16. Close up of "flat horns" of the *P. bifurcatum.*

17. Young specimen of *P. angolense.*

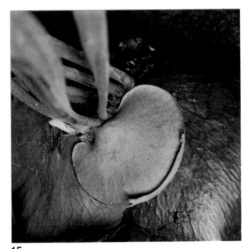

15

14

16   17

Foliage plants

Aspidistra

The Aspidistra is a common plant, once very popular in every home. It is out of style—being associated with the Victorian era.

Origins. It is native to the Far East (Japan, China) and was imported in the first decades of 19th Century. It has met much enthusiasm on account of its easy culture and its sturdiness that justify the name given to it by the British: Iron Plant.

Morphology. The *Aspidistra* genus belong to the Liliaceae family. It has few species of which *A. elatior* is the best known. *Aspidistra* plants are herbaceous, rhizomatous, with numerous acaulous, large, persistent leaves, oblong-lanceolate, leathery, dark green, and striped with white in some cultivars. The bell-shaped flowers are blue or bluish-violet, almost sessile, not ornamental and are a scientific curiosity since they have, contrary to the Liliaceae in general, 8 stamens and an ovary with 4 locules. The fruit is a globose berry with numerous seeds.

Cultivation. It is well known and only used as a foliage plant. Very resistant to the worst conditions of humidity, dust, and light, it will also tolerate frost. It can therefore be used in regions with a mild climate outdoors, where it is suitable for thickets and borders in cool and shaded areas of the garden. It is very vigorous and grows in any type of soil. Propagation is performed in spring by division of the clumps, with the precaution that each piece of rhizome must bear at least one leaf. The single segments are planted 3 or 4 per pot and new root development is favored in warm conditions.

Species and varieties. The only species that interest us is the *A. elatior*. Garden varieties are not well classified. They are distinguished by the different color of the leaves that appear variegated or dotted.

18. The traditional *Aspidistra elatior* with its large, shiny leaves.

21

20 22

23

Aralias

This name has been given to several plants that botanically now belong to different genera such as *Fatsia, Dizygotheca, Panax, Polyscias,* and others. Considering the nature of the present volume, we will not get involved in the morphological differences, but will limit ourselves to a brief consideration of those species that are of interest from the ornamental gardening point of view. These genera belong to the Araliaceae family.

Morphology.   Their appearance is shrubby or as small trees with palmate, compound digitate leaves that are almost linear in some forms or whole. The inflorescence is globose, mostly umbrella-shaped, with tiny flowers of no ornamental value. The fruit is a berry.

In our environment they are of interest for decorating houses and offices, where, if given attention, they last a long time. They can also be used in groups for temporary decoration of gardens during the summer season.

Cultivation.   They are propagated by seed or by cuttings, and even by grafting and layering.

They are plants suited for a temperate greenhouse with an optimum around 58°F. They grow best in a diffused light. As far as the soil is concerned, they are not demanding, but a good soil mixture can include leaf mold, top soil, and sand. Irrigation should be frequent, but not abundant.

Species and varieties.   *Fatsia japonica* is a widely dispersed tree, very popular for the elegance of its large leaves, particularly charming in the *variegata* variety, spotted with yellow or white. Propagation is by seed or by cuttings.

Dizygotheca elegantissima is a plant worthy of its name because of the light beauty of its leaves that are thin and waxy. It is generally propagated by grafting on *Fatsia japonica* or *Oreopanax reticulatum,* or by cuttings, under glass.

Polyscias fruticosa with the *plumata* variety; *P. Guilfoylei,* with the *laciniata, Victoria,* and *monstrosa* varieties; and *P. rumphiana* are pretty house plants even though they are not as well known as the *Fatsia.*

Fatshedera Lizei is a hybrid between the *Fatsia* and *Hedera.* It is evergreen, tolerates indoor conditions, and is very popular, but it deserves even greater use since it has an easy culture and is attractive.

---

19. *Fatsia japonica,* sometimes incorrectly called *Aralia japonica* var. *sieboldii.*

20. *Fatsia japonica* var. *Moseri.*

21. A branch of *Fatshedera Lizei.*

22. The lacy appearance of the leaves of *Dizygotheca elegantissima.*

23. Close up of leaves of *Dizygotheca.*

24. *Fatsia japonica,* a young seedling.

24

25

26

27

2

Asparagus

The name certainly brings to our mind the memory of delicious dishes that gourmets prepare in various ways for the joy of food lovers. Yet we will skip the edible species that is only used for the table in order to call attention to those cultivated as greenhouse and house plants.

Origins. These plants are of different origins: some species are from the Mediterranean region; some come from Siberia, the Orient, and from South Africa.

The *Asparagus* genus belongs to the Liliaceae family and includes about 300 species.

Morphology. They are all perennial herbaceous plants, with fleshy roots and runners or climbing stems. Numerous branchlets, whose configurations and development vary with each species, function as leaves. The axillary or terminal flowers are arranged in racemes and are small. The fruit is a berry containing globose and flattened seeds.

Cultivation. Skipping the common garden asparagus, numerous plants of these are culti-

vated in greehouses, both for the elegant decorative effect they provide when set in pots and as a source of foliage which can be cut for floral arrangements. They are easy to grow and can be propagated by seeds or by division. They are tolerant as far as the soil is concerned, but they are injured by cold.

Species and varieties. The species grown as ornamentals are:

A. verticillatus, used for covering walls and fences.

A. Sprengeri, cultivated outdoors in the South and under glass in the North.

A. asparagoides, used by florists especially in the myrtifolius cultivar.

A. plumosus (Asparagus fern), (with the cultivars *tenuissimus, compactus, nanus,* and others) is the most used species for floral decorations and is cultivated commercially.

25. Note the airiness of the *Asparagus plumosus* var. *nanus.*

26. Close up of *Asparagus plumosus.*

27. Fruits of *Asparagus Sprengeri.*

31

32

Philodendron

The Greek roots of the name (*phileo* = to love and *dendron* = tree) describes the natural habit of this plant that is a climbing vine.

Origins. Native to tropical forests of South America, they represent a characteristic plant of the undergrowth from which they emerge attaching themselves to taller trees by their adventitious roots. Introduced in cultivation more than a century ago, they are cultivated for the beauty of their leaves and for the elegant appearance that makes them desirable for greenhouses and houses.

The *Philodendrons* are Monocotyledons belonging to the family of the Araceae. The number of the classified species is controversial, but according to recent studies is close to 100.

Morphology. Herbaceous and vining plants, they have a thick stem with long internodes and are provided with numerous and thick aerial roots. The leaves are large, often very large, shiny, and leathery. Shape of the leaves is variable, and can be cordate, oval, sagittate, or pole-shaped, with entire, lobate, or pinnate margins. The flowers (blossoms develop in greenhouses on large specimens) are unisexual, gathered into a spadix inflorescence wrapped by a gaudy spathe that is creamy-white, pinkish, or yellowish. The single fruits are fleshy berries.

Cultivation. The *Philodendrons* are plants with great ornamental value, both for house and greenhouse, and their use continues to increase. Their cultivation in greenhouses with a high humidity is very easy. They are grown in pots according to the plant size and ultimate use. The soil may be a mixture of loam, organic matter, and sand.

They prefer diffused light and it is best to avoid strong or cold drafts. The propagation is by cuttings, and roots develop in a warm humid environment. Layering is also possible but it is done less frequently. Tip cuttings obtained from the apex make the most attractive plants.

Species and varieties. The species of *Philodendrons* and the cultivars are many. Among the familar ones is *P. scandens* (Sweetheart Vine), well-known for its tolerance to indoor conditions, with its varieties *variegatum* and *aureo-variegatum.*

Also worthy of mention are: *P. Selloum,* with large, oval, oblong leaves; *P. bipinnatifidum,* that is bushy and not climbing; *P. erubescens,* admired for the oval shape and the pink undercolor of the leaves.

The *Monstera deliciosa* belongs to the Araceae and can commonly be mistaken for *Philodendron pertusum.* It has an equally decorative value and similar culture.

34

28. *Monstera deliciosa,* in hydroponic culture.

29. Related to the *Philodendrons* are the *Scindapsus aureua,* cv. "Marble Queen."

30, 31. A popular house plant is *Philodendron scandens* with the elegant, heart-shaped leaves emphasized in the illustration.

32. Cutting of *Philodendron scandens;* the aerial roots coming out of the node are evident.

33. A nice specimen of *Philodendron Selloum.*

34. *Monstera deliciosa,* pretty plant of the Araceae family, adhering to the stone wall of a greenhouse.

35

37

36

39

Begonias

A chapter would not be enough, but rather a whole volume would be fitting for these plants that are well known for the beauty of their leaves, the grace and abundance of their blooms, and the variability in shapes that make them excellent plants for house decoration, gardens, and for long-lasting flower beds.

Origins. All species of the *Begonia* genus that are cultivated originated in the American and Asiatic tropics, from where they were imported to Europe first in 1770. A few, like the *B. veitchii,* came from the Andes at more than 13,000 feet.

It is the most important genus of the Begoniaceae family, to which it gives its name. The number of species is controversial, but there are probably more than 500.

Morphology. These are herbaceous or slightly shrubby plants with a succulent appearance. Their stem can be extensively branched or reduced to a rhizome, to a tuber, or to a bulb-like tuber. The leaves are stalked, alternate, and often asymmetric; they are of various shapes including orbicular, reniform, peltate, and palmate; they can also be bristly, especially on the underside, with a whole or toothed margin. Almost all species have leaves with beautiful colors that include all variations of green, from a light to a very dark shade, with metallic reflections, or purple of different intensity and with variegations and designs of interesting effect.

The sexual flowers are very small in some species, but abundant; in others, they are large and showy, in white, pink, red, or yellow. The fruits are winged capsules with many tiny seeds.

Begonias interest us as ornamental house and garden plants for their leaves, for their flowers or for both leaves and flowers.

Cultivation. The cultivation of begonias is not difficult and, although there are differences according to the species, the soil, light, temperature, and water demands are common to all.

The basis for a good begonia cultivation is provided by an environment that is warm and humid, and in which the plants receive diffused light, soil rich in organic matter or peat, or leaf mold and sand, and abundant watering.

Begonias are propagated by seed and by cuttings of a branch or a leaf, or even, in some species, by division of the rhizomes or of the tubers. Seed is used for *Begonia semperflorens,* the well-known everblooming begonia used for flower beds and borders. Seed is planted in fall or in spring, in pots under glass and without covering. The seedlings must be transplanted.

The cutting of a leaf or a shoot is commonly used because of the ability of begonias to regenerate tissues easily; the cuttings root faithfully, reproducing the mother plant. Propagation by division of rhizomes and tubers is peculiar to a few species, such as *B. tuberhybrida.*

Species and varieties. Due to lack of space, attention is called to only a few of the most common species emphasizing, though, that many others deserve the attention of the loving flower-grower.

B. semperflorens, or garden begonia, is used in borders, flower beds, carpet bedding, and for pot plants. It has variable shapes and color with hundreds of varieties and hybrids that are increasing every year. Excellent cultivars include Linda, Scarletta, Matador, Pink Pearl, Viva, and Indian Maid.

B. tuberhybrida is the well-known tuberous begonia that embellishes terraces and grows well even in semi-shaded flower beds, producing bloom with warm and luminous shades from June to November, in numerous varieties with single and double flowers that may be erect or pendulous, cristate, or fringed. Seed of these types is sold according to flower color or as a mixture.

B. Rex, B. asplenifolia, B. metallica, and *B. socotrana* ("Gloire de Lorraine") are all cultivated for their magnificent and variously colored foliage.

---

35. The beautiful, variegated foliage of the *Begonia Rex,* cultivar "Iron Cross."

36. Young potted plant of *Begonia semperflorens, cv* "Vernon."

37-38 Flowers of *Begonia tuberhybrida,* the bulbous begonia.

39. Single flower of *Begonia,* cv. "Vernon."

40. *Begonia Scharffii* flowers.

42

41. *Peperomia caperata* in flower.

42. Leaf cutting of *Peperomia caperata* with a sprout; on the right, a leaf cutting just made.

43. Pot with *Peperomia caperata*.

44. *Peperomia griseo argentea*.

45. Leaf cutting of *Peperomia griseo argentea*.

43

44

45

eperomias

These plants, native to tropical regions (Bra- , Peru, Argentina), were introduced in the sec- d half of the nineteenth century.
The genus *Peperomia* belongs to the Pipera- ae family. Its name means "pepper-like" in- cating a certain similarity with the genus, per. There are about 100 species.

orphology. They are evergreen herba- ous plants, with a radical leaf arrangement d a short stem that is barely developed; the ernate fleshy leaves are opposite or verticil- e, have an entire margin, cordiform or unded acuminate, and frequently have inter- ing variegations. Peculiar and interesting are

the clustered inflorescences that look like "mouse tails," with a white cream color. The flowers are insignificant as far as decoration is concerned, and the same is true for the fruits that are little berries with thin pericarps.

Cultivation. The decorative value of the leaves, the facility of cultivation in the green- house, and the long duration in houses make peperomias much appreciated. The small size and the modest development of the plant sug- gests cultivation in little pots with a soil mixture of loam, peat or organic matter, and sand. To get good results, it is necessary to reserve a shaded location and to avoid excessive watering.

Peperomias can be propagated by seed which should be scattered in pots, in fine, loose soil. Commonly though, the plants are propagated by cuttings in spring. The little segments of stems with a leaf are placed in sand in a propagation greenhouse or frame; they will need to be con- stantly shaded and watered.

Species and varieties. Among the most popular peperomias are: *Peperomia ob- tusifolia,* with green leaves and marginal dark spots; *P. marmorata* and *P. verschaffeltii,* with green, marbled leaves; *P. argyroneura,* with green leaves and silver stripes; *P. caperata,* with green and fleshy leaves.

46

48

50

Rubber plants

The *Ficus* are among the most well known, widely used and best loved of house plants. Their popularity is certainly derived from the decorativeness of the plant whose leaves, although somewhat stiff, are nonetheless beautiful.

Origins. The *Ficus* are native to Central and South America and Asia. Those most commonly cultivated as decorative plants have been imported from India and Malaysia.

The *Ficus* belong to the Moraceae family and include more than 600 species.

Morphology. These can be trees; or shrubby, herbaceous and climbing plants. The tall *Ficus* often have aerial adventitious roots that grow to the ground forming a colonnade around the main stem. Others have long flat roots shaped like supports around the plant. Their leaves are lobate or entire, plain or wavy, alternate and almost always persistent, leathery, with evident veins. Sometimes different leaf shapes are found in the same plant. The width of the leaves varies from species to species and in them stipules that cover the terminal buds are always present.

Ficus are mainly monoecious plants, with a characteristic inflorescence shaped like a swollen axis that is fleshy, concave, and composed of unisexual sessile flowers. The fruits are achenes. All *Ficus* secrete a white latex that is thick and often caustic.

The Biblical Sycomorous *(Ficus Sycomorous)*

and the common fig *(Ficus carica)* are used fc their fruit. Others produce types of latex used fc making lacquers.

Cultivation. These plants are propagate in a hot and shaded greenhouse with an optim; temperature around 65°F and high humidit; They can be propagated by tip cuttings or ste; cuttings. The cuttings root in a warm, moi; environment. Once the roots have taken, pot th cuttings in fertile and loose soil composed three parts of organic matter, two parts of to soil, and one part of sand.

Species and varieties. The most wel known species is *F. elastica* (Indian Rubbe Plant) and its cultivar *decora,* which has da; green, rigid, oblong, lanceolate leaves enclos; in the bud by a red sheath.

F. lyrata is a pretty plant, commonly call; Fiddleleaf Fig because of the characterist shape of the leaves that look like a violin a; may reach 15 inches in length.

Worthy of mention is *F. diversifolia* (Mistl toe Fig), that demonstrates heterophylly a; bears at the axil of the leaves numerous yello; berries which increase its decorative value.

Finally, the *F. pumila* (Creeping Fig), mo; commonly known as *F. repens,* has a climbi; stem and is suitable for eovering an entire w; in a greenhouse; it has small, leathery leav; which are heterophyllous on the terminal flo; ering branches.

51

52

53

54

55

Dracaenas

From tropical Africa, from islands of the Indian Ocean, and from Central America, we have imported these plants, some of which are extremely elegant for their habit of growth and attractive foliage. They are considered among the best kinds for house decoration, as they match in their beauty the tolerance to environmental conditions of modern houses.

These Monocotyldeons belong to the Liliaceae family and the genus *Dracaena* has about 50 species, half of which are of interest. The most cultivated species will be discussed here.

Morphology. These shrubby plants can become trees on maturity. The cultivated species develop at a moderate rate, and have a rigid and erect stem which is covered with long, sessile or largely-stalked, ensiform or ovate, lanceolate or elliptical leaves. The leaves are an attractive green and may be uniform or striped with white. The infloresences are numerous in a head or a cluster, composed of small single flowers having a whitish-green or yellowish-green color, and are of only little value ornamentally. The fruit is a berry with three ovules.

Until 1868, the year in which it was destroyed by a violent storm, a specimen of *Dracaena Draco,* uprooted in Tenerife, was considered to be one of the largest trees (measuring 46 feet in circumference) and one of the oldest (the age was appraised at 6,000 years). From trees of this species in their native countries, a resin is obtained that is used both in the preparation of varnishes and for therapeutic purposes.

Cultivation. Dracaenas are greatly appreciated for their ornamental qualities and have established themselves in a favorable position among the various ornamental indoor plants.

Dracaenas are cultivated in a temperate or warm greenhouse at from 55 to 60° F. They may be reproduced by seed but are more commonly propagated by cuttings or by air layering. They grow best in a light fertile soil, that can be made of one part peat and one part loam, mixed with one-half part sand.

Species and varieties. Among the most cultivated species, the following is especially fine: *Dracaena deremensis,* which is particularly attractive, with graceful green leaves having silver stripes.

Also worthy of note are: *D. fragrans* in the varieties *Lindenii* and *Massangeana; D. Hookeriana; D. Goldieana;* and *D. Godseffiana,* appreciated for its shrubby appearance and its dark green spiraled leaves which are spotted in a light color.

Last is mentioned the two beautiful species that belong to the genus *Cordyline,* but which are commonly called dracaenas; they are fine plants with brightly colored leaves and are named *Cordyline terminalis* and *Cordyline indivisa,* with long and narrow leaves and elegant stand.

46. Cuttings of *Ficus* on the bench of a propagation greenhouse.

47. *Ficus repens:* in the foreground a fertile branch presenting the phenomenon of heterophylly (leaves of different shapes).

48. *Ficus repens* on the wall of a greenhouse.

49. *Ficus elastica:* the cutting has originated a new plant.

50. *F. pandurata.*

51. *Dracaena Draco:* young plant in a pot.

52. *Cordyline indivisa,* formerly known as *Dracaena indivisa.*

53. *Dracaena deremensis* var. *Warneckii.*

54. Young tip cutting of *Dracaena deremensis.*

55. Group of *Dracaena arborea.*

56

57

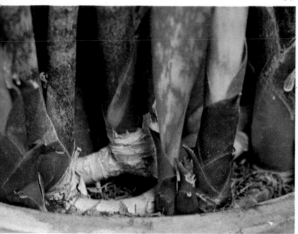

59

61

Sanservierias

Dedicated to Raymond of Sangrio, Prince of Sansevero, this genus contains some of the most widely-used species for indoor decoration.

Origins. Sansevierias grow natively in regions of tropical and subtropical Africa and even of India.

The genus *Sanseviera* belongs to the Liliaceae family.

Morphology. These are perennial herbaceous plants (a few species are woody); they grow in clumps and have a thick and short rhizome from which a very short stem develops. The leaves, which represent a large part of the

plant, are thick, leathery, and fibrous. They range in length from a very few inches to 3 feet, have flat or slightly concave sides that are also ensiform, and are gray-greenish or green, and spotted or striped with clear transversal lines. A few species have cylindrical and very peculiar leaves. The flowers, carried by long scapes in a large number, are in clusters and have a tubular shape with a perianth of 6 greenish-white petals; they are strongly scented, but do not have any ornamental value.

In their native countries they are used for the strong fiber from their leaves which is suited for the weaving of ropes.

Cultivation. The cultivation of sanse erias is done in temperate greenhouses. The s of the pots will be rather heavy; it is formed mixing one part loam and one part organic ma ter with one-half part sand. It is necessary control the temperature, which must never below 45 to 50° F (at 43° sansevierias are jured). They do not need particular care. Mode ate waterings must be given in winter. summer they can be located in warm and we lighted locations.

Propagation is by division of the clumps, spring. It is also possible to use a leaf cutting, b the characteristic variegation is not retaine

Aphelandras (Zebra plants)

Aphelandras are attractive both for their leaves and for their flowers; therefore they should never be absent from an amateur greenhouse. They were imported more than a century ago from Mexico and from Brazil.

Morphology. Because of the stripes on their leaves, they have also been called "zebra plants." Aphelandras are evergreen, shrubby or herbaceous, but sturdy plants, belonging to the Acanthaceae family and included in the genus *Aphelandra.* There are about 80 species of which about 10 are of interest as ornamentls.

They have opposite, simple, ovate-lanceolate, rigid, pinnate-veined leaves that have a bright green color striped with white or yellow; the underside is often reddish. The inflorescence is an erect, terminal cluster with a characteristic pyramidal shape and has "tiled" bracts that are red or yellow. The single flowers are sessile, bilabiate, and tubular and display different colors: yellow, red, orange. The fruit is a dehiscent capsule containing 4 seeds.

Cultivation. Aphelandras, in recent years, have emerged from their role as botanical peculiarities and have proved to be excellent house plants. They reproduce by seed and are easily propagated by cuttings of young shoots. They are demanding as far as the soil is concerned because they prefer a well-fertilized soil with well-decomposed organic matter.

They are cultivated in a warm greenhouse (only a few species, like the *Aphelandra aurantiaca,* can adjust itself to a temperate greenhouse) at 72 to 77°F with high humidity. After blooming, for a period of rest, they are placed in a 41–43°F environment, and their watering is limited. They should be repotted yearly.

Species and varieties. The most commonly-cultivated aphelandras belong to the species *A. squarrosa,* with green shiny leaves having veins emphasized by white and yellow stripes; the inflorescence has bracts and flowers in the same dark yellow color. The cultivar *Louisae* is one of the best pot plants.

The *A. aurantiaca,* hardier in regard to temperature requirements, has a duller and uniform green color, and an orange inflorescence. Interesting also are *A. fascinator* and *A. tetragona,* which are shrubby and very pretty species with scarlet inflorescences.

63

64

e thick clumps should be repotted every year, ward the end of spring, using a pot that is ger than the previous one; a good liquid fertiltion will favor the growth of new leaves.

pecies and varieties. The most widespread species is *Sansevieria zylanica,* cortly known as *S. trifasciata,* of which the urentii variety, with green leaves that are graytiped and have yellow edges, is the most autiful.

The *S. hahnii,* Birds' Nest Sansevieria, is ther short and has rosette leaves; and the *S. lindrica* species has cylindrical leaves.

56. The small and pretty *Sansevieria hahnii* in the pot.

57. Young sprouts of *Sansevieria hahnii.*

58. Sprout of *Sansevieria* originated by a cutting.

59. Close up of the rhizome of *Sansevieria trifasciata.*

60. *Sansevieria hahnii.*

61. *Sansevieria trifasciata* var. *Laurentii* in hydroponic culture.

62. Leaf cuttings of *Sansevieria trifasciata* var. *Laurentii.*

63-64. The attractive leaves of the *Aphelandra squarrosa.*

65

66

Aechmeas

These very elegant plants are undoubtedly destined to increase in popularity and to be incorporated more frequently in interior decorating schemes.

Origins. The *Aechmeas* are plants characteristic of the tropical and subtropical flora of South America and have become the most popular of all bromelaids.

The *Aechmea* genus belongs to the Bromeliaceae family, rich in numerous greenhouse and house plants. The most famous representative of the family is *Ananas comosus,* the pineapple.

The *Aechmea* species includes about sixty known members, only a few of which are cultivated. However, there is an ever-growing number of hybrids.

Morphology. The *Aechmeas* attract attention for their rigid, opened, spiny, and curved leaves, which are marbled or striped with white, and are sometimes pinkish on the lower surface.

The inflorescence, a cluster located in the center of the rosette of leaves, has single flowers in the axil of colored bracts. The fruit are fleshy, ornamental berries.

Cultivation. Exclusively cultivated for the indoors, these plants have stimulated the flower growers' interst. Cultivation is in a temperate greenhouse, in a small pot, since the root development of the *Aechmeas* is small. This plant demands the use of a particularly suitable soil medium that can be made of, for example, three parts organic matter, one-half part of sand and sphagnum, and one part of good top soil.

Propagation may be by seed, but it is preferable to utilize the shoots that form at the base of the plant. The best time to divide is late spring. The shoots are potted and kept at 80 to 85°F until the roots take. The adult plants require a temperate greenhouse, abundant but indirect light, and frequent watering.

Species and varieties. The most culti-

vated species of *Aechmeas* are *A. fasciata* wi dark blue flowers and bracts, and *A. fulgen* with longer leaves and purple flowers with sca let sepals.

Other Bromeliaceae. Very close sy tematically to the *Aechmeas,* and often co fused among each other, are other genera Bromeliaceae that are of great interest for t beauty of their leaves and flowers. Examples a *Bilbergia, Vriesia, Tillandsia, Nidulariu Cryptanthus, Neoregelia, Gusmania.* They have requirements similar to those described f *Aechmeas* and are capable of attracting our terest and our surprised admiration.

65. *Aechmeas fulgens* with its elegant foliage a beautiful inflorescence.

66. Another pretty *Aechmea.*

67. Flower of *Aechmea.*

68, 69. Very similar to the *Aechmea* are oth Bromeliaceae such as the *Neoregelia* (68) and t *Gusmania* (69).

68

Caladium

The elegant shape of the leaves and the variety of colors which they display place these plants among those most commonly used in the greenhouse and in houses, where, even though they do not last for a long time, they bestow a note of marked refinement.

Origins. The *Caladium* are native of warm humid forests of Brazil, where they grow naturally as an undergrowth in woods, especially along the rivers and streams. They were introduced in Europe in the second half of the eighteenth century and have since attracted great interest among floriculturists. Much attention has been focused on them by the general public at expositions.

Caladium is a genus of the Araceae family that includes peculiar and interesting plants. It has many species and numerous hybrids.

Morphology. They are herbaceous plants with a tuberous rhizome from which the leaves develop. The leaves have long stalks, are mostly sagittate or sagittate-cordate shape but can even be eliptical-ovate, and are as large as 24 inches with evident veins. The colors, which make the leaves extremely beautiful, vary from pink to crimson to red and are concentrated in the center with the margin remaining more or less marbled or dotted.

The spadix inflorescence is wrapped by a white spathe and is scented. The fruits are whitish berries, that fall on reaching maturity.

Cultivation. As already mentioned, the *Caladium* are plants of a great interest for greenhouses and for outdoor decoration. Their cultivation is successful if one carefully creates all the conditions characteristic of their original habitat, which is only possible in the greenhouse. The pots are carried dry over winter at a temperature of about 60°F. Between January and April, the soil around the tuber is cleaned off and the young buds that are not yet developed are planted in a mixture of leaf mold, top soil, and sand, and then placed in the greenhouse at 65 to 70°F, watering heavily. Once the development of the first leaf has taken place, each young plant will need to be potted and these young plants will be kept in a shaded greenhouse where they are supplied with water. In September, waterings will become less frequent until the beginning of the complete rest of the plant that will be apparent by the fall of the leaves.

Propagation can take place by means of the little tubers. The *Caladium* are also reproduced by seeds; in this case, the colors of the leaves will appear after the fifth or sixth leaf develops.

Species and varieties. The best-known and most widely-grown species is the *Caladium bicolor,* with bright red leaves in the center and green around the borders.

Also well known are *C. picturatum* and *C. Schomburgkii,* including numerous cultivars.

Having a smaller size, with ovate, oblong, green-spotted leaves, but equally pretty, is the species *C. Humboldtii.*

---

70. Beautiful and flashy leaves of *Caladium bicolor.*

71. Note the variation in the leaves of different cultivars of *Caladium.*

Croton

Here are the plants commonly called Crotons; they are attractive plants that are cultivated in greenhouses for decoration indoors. Botanically, they belong to the genus *Codiaeum* and are appreciated because of the bright colors of their leaves and, often, of their stems.

Origins.   Native of Malaysian islands, they were imported in the beginning of 1800 and since that time have aroused vivid interest and promoted intense activity in selection and hybridization.

The *Codiaeum* genus belongs to the Euphorbiaceae family. Six species are known of which only *Codiaeum variegatum* is interesting to the gardener.

Morphology.   These small trees or shrubby plants have persistent, alternate, simple leaves with an entire or lobate margin which demonstrate bright and changeable colors. When the plants are young, the leaves are green and yellow; when the plants mature, red may be the main leaf color, although the entire range of shades of yellow, orange, and red may be included in different combinations. The unisexual flowers, in an axillary raceme, do not offer any ornamental value.

Cultivation.   In their original habitat, the *Codiaeum* grow easily, developing until they form thick and strong bushes. They are referred to as "variegated laurel" by the English. These are exclusively plants for the hot and humid greenhouse, and require a winter temperature of from 65 to 68°F. In frost-free areas, they grow outdoors. They need abundant, but diffused, light and high humidity.

The soil is important for maintaining the plant in the best conditions. We suggest a mixture of four parts organic matter, one part good top soil, and one-half part sand.

Propagation is by cuttings. Layering is also used especially to rejuvenate old plants that have been deprived of leaves at the base. The cuttings are taken during late winter and spring, are rooted in sand, and then potted.

Species and varieties.   The only species with a garden interest is *C. variegatum*. The garden varieties are numerous and can be separated into two categories: those with entire leaves and those with lobate leaves.

72. Among the prettiest house plants, the *Codiaeum*, commonly named *Croton,* cultivar "Clipper."

73. *Codiaeum variegatum* var. *contorta,* with spiraled leaves.

Dieffenbachia

This plant is named in honor of J. F. Dieffenbach, a German botanist who was for many years, around 1800, the supervisor of the castle of Schönbrunn. The plant is a native of tropical America (Brazil, Venezuela, Equador, and Colombia) and has been widely distributed as a greenhouse plant and for indoor decoration.

The genus *Dieffenbachia* includes about 12 species and belongs to the Araceae family that includes many other foliage plants (*Philodendron, Caladium,* etc.) which are valuable because of the beauty of their leaves.

Morphology. They are herbaceous, shrubby plants with a creeping or erect, succulent stem. The leaves are carried by long semicylindrical stalks that are encased for half of their length by a sheath. The leaves are large with an oblong shape, and are basically green, but show a variable degree of spotting or marking in yellow or gray-green; they have prominent veins. The inflorescence is a spadix with an oblong and persistent spathe and does not have any special ornamental value. The juice of the plant is highly toxic.

Cultivation. As has been mentioned, these plants are of great interest because of the beauty of their leaves and are much used for interior decoration. They have a tendency to lose their basal leaves after months indoors.

Their cultivation demands temperatures around 65 to 68°F, a high humidity, and the avoidance of frequent changes in temperature.

They are propagated by seed, but are usually propagated by cutting or layers, made in the greenhouse from February to March. The soil used must be loose and light textured and can be a mixture of three parts organic matter and one part top soil with a little bit of sand.

At the beginning of spring each year, the plants are repotted.

Once they are taken into the house, be sure to place the plants under diffused light in as cool a location as possible.

Species and varieties. There are several garden varieties available on the market; two are *Dieffenbachia picta* and *D. Seguine.*

74-75. Two varieties of *Dieffenbachia picta: arvida* (74) and *superba* (75).

74

Calatheas and marantas

The magnificence of nature can be admired in a sunset on the sea, in an alpine landscape, or even more simply by observing the delicate embroidery on the leaves of these very pretty plants.

Origins. Both are native to tropical regions of South America, and are located along the large rivers. They have proved themselves to be excellent candidates for house plants and for large indoor displays.

The *Calathea* and *Maranta* genera both belong to the *Marantaceae* family.

Morphology. They are perennial herbaceous plants that are rhizomatous and are either almost deprived of aerial stems or have very short one, as in the case of *Maranta*.

The leaves, large in *Calatheas* and smaller in *Marantas,* are on long stalks with a green background, and are variously shaped, colored, or have very bright and regular stripes. The lower surface is almost always uniformly reddish or it reproduces, in different shades, the same design that is on the upper surface. The flower and the fruit are necessary to make the botanical identification, but do not have any ornamental value.

If we exclude *Maranta arundinacea* that is cultivated in India and Oceania, but mainly in Central America for arrowroot starch, the other species have ornamental value for greenhouses, as house plants, and for gardens in the tropics.

Cultivation. They are warm temperature plants that almost all require a 75–80°F temperature, a high humidity, and reduced light. These, of course, represent the conditions peculiar to their original environment.

Calathea is more sensitive to strong light; the *Maranta* is more tolerant.

They are propagated in spring by division of the clumps and of the rhizomes; reproduction by seed is utilized only by breeders.

They grow best in a mixture that is rich in organic matter and can be made of six parts organic matter and two parts top soil to one part sand. During the vegetative period they need frequent watering that will be reduced from November to February, the period during which the plants are less active in growth.

Species and varieties. Among the best-known species, are:

Calathea Mackoyana, coming from Brazil, is called by the English "peacock plant" because of the colors of the leaves.

C. ornata, native to Columbia, is vigorous and has large elliptical leaves.

C. roseo-picta, from Brazil is smaller size

C. Veitchiana, from Peru, has large leav with a purple coloration on the lower surfa

C. zebrina, with elegant stripes, does well a temperate greenhouse.

They are all excellent plants that go well wi *Maranta bicolor* and *M. leuconeura,* the Pray Plant, and its varieties *Massangeana* and *K choveana.*

---

76. The delicate embroidery in the leaves of *Mara. leuconeura,* var. *Kerchoveana.*

77. Leaf of *Calathea insignis.*

78. *Calathea Mackoyana,* the "peacock plant."

Palms

*The palms recall mysterious and exotic landscapes where the sea and sandy beaches represent a
natural background for human activities which are accompanied by the rhythmic sound of the waves.
They may remind us of a joyful spot for the annual vacation.
Many kinds are cultivated because they are excellent for the greenhouse, for the house, and
generally are suited for interior decoration. They are easy to cultivate and have few demands. In this
book we will describe some of the most popular palms, mentioning also some other species worthy
of attention.*

Kentia palms or howea

79

The *Kentias,* properly classified as a species of
the genus *Howea,* even if the old name is still
used, are the most important palms for indoor
use and special decoration.

They are the pride of many greenhouses and
botanical gardens where they are always admired.

Origins. Once classified in the genus
Kentia, they are now classified in the genus
Howea: Palmaceae family.

They are native of the Lord Howe Islands, in
the Pacific, and include only two species, *H.
Belmoreana* and *H. Forsteriana.*

Morphology. They are plants which
become large in their native habitat and have
upright stems that may reach 35 feet or more.
Characteristic is the presence of protruding
roots with the base thickened by the stem itself.

They present terminal, large, numerous, pin-
natafid, semi-pendulous leaves. The infloresences are spadix shaped, are 30 to 40 inches
long, and are composed of flowers in groups of
three. The fruit is a fibrous drupe.

Cultivation. *Kentias* are showy plants
used in houses and, more often, in churches,
theaters, and public buildings.

They are produced by seed that is rather slow
to germinate and requires a loose and warm soil.

The young plants are transplanted according to
their growth, sometimes using two or more
plants to a pot. Where the climate is frost free,
they are cultivated in nursery beds and transplanted as needed to give them the space de-
manded for their development. They grow in
organic matter mixed with a good top soil and
sand.

Once they have reached the commercial stage,
they are potted for interior use. Instead of repotting adult plants, make additions of top soil.
When they are kept in the greenhouse, they are
shaded and require frequent watering.

Species and varieties. The two species
of *Howea* are: *H. Belmoreana,* which is of moderate size, has large and greatly arched leaves as
long as 6 feet, with numerous pointed leaf segments; and *H. Forsteriana,* which can reach 60
feet in height and whose leaves are larger than
the other species, with less numerous, but larger,
leaf segments.

80

79. Young specimen of the *Howea Forsteriana.*

80. Close up of *Howea Forsteriana.*

81. A pretty palm: the *Collinia elegans* as undergrowth in a forest (see page 39).

82. Palms of the species *Chamaerops humilis* (See
page 38).

81   82

83

Chamaerops—Rhapis—Cocos

In the chapter dedicated to the palms, brief mention is necessary of those genera that offer excellent choices for the greenhouse and house, and even for garden plants.

Chamaerops. Only one species exists, the St. Peter Palm or *C. humilis.* It is cultivated in the greenhouse, can adjust itself to various environments, can endure a bright sun exposure and cool temperatures. It is also tolerant to drought and is most suitable for decorating. Characteristic are the large, palmate leaves.

Rhapis. One of the fan-palms, so-called because of the shape of its leaves, it has a modest development and a matted appearance, is excellent for house decoration, where it can tolerate unfavorable conditions. Where frost-free climates prevail, it can be grown in the garden.

Cocos. A well-known plant is the species *C. nucifera,* the coconut, which is cultivated for its fruit and is familiar on account of the related *Arecastrum Romanzoffianum,* particularly in the variety *Australe,* and *Syagrus Weddelliana.*

These were previously classified as *Cocos a* are used in gardening and are among the pret est palms, with long, pinnate and very lig leaves. They require warm temperature and f tile soil. The *Cocos* genus includes only t coconut, which is never grown indoors.

83-84. *Phoenix canariensis* in a pot and in a gr along the Mediterranean coast.

85. The date palm: *Phoenix dactylifera.*

86. *Cocos nucifera* in its natural environment.

87 88

89 90

Chamaedoreas

This plant is native to Mexico and the countries of Central and South America. The name, deriving from Greek, means dwarf gift and suggests the small size of this plant. *Chamaedoreas* are very elegant and are therefore used in house decoration.

Morphology. The genus *Chamaedorea* belongs to the Palmaceae. It includes about 70 species, of which about 10 are in the nursery trade.

They are small, erect, or procumbent palms, almost always bushy and often with a reed-like appearance. The leaves are mostly pinnatifid, sometimes simple. They are dioecious plants which means that the male and female flowers are on different plants. The fruit is a small, dry, or fleshy berry.

Cultivation. With the exception of *Chamaedorea Pacaya* and of *C. Tepejilote*, whose male inflorescences are used in Central America as a vegetable, the *Chamaedoreas* are cultivated only for use as house plants.

Like all palms, they can be easily reproduced by seed in the greenhouse in any season. Use fresh seed that still maintains its germination ability, which is lost as the seed dries out. This is true for all the cultivated palms. Use a pot which has a cylindrical shape and is deep because of the tendency of the roots to grow downward.

This plant prefers diffused light. The *Chamaedoreas* are not particularly demanding for water, but should be watered regularly. For soil, use a mixture of five parts organic matter and two parts top soil to one part sand. Fertilize adult plants in the spring. They grow well in a temperate green-house.

Species and varieties. Among the most popular is the related *Collinia elegans* that is very familiar and very attractive; it is the smallest among the cultivated palms. It has dainty foliage and pinnate leaves that are as long as 30 cms.

Chamaedorea elatior is excellent for its tolerance to cold which allows it to live in the open ground in frost-free areas.

C. Ernesti Augustii has simple leaves.

Phoenix

Phoenix dactylifera, the date palm, is the classical palm referred to in the Old and New Testaments and known for its symbolism of martyrdom because of its use when Jesus triumphantly entered Jerusalem. It has also always been well known as a fruit and is sometimes used as an ornamental plant.

Morphology. The genus *Phoenix* belongs to the *Palmaceae* family and includes about 12 species. They are mostly plants having tall stems, whose upper stem near the top is covered with the base of the stalks of the old leaves that have fallen. They have very large leaves that are pinnate, with whole, rigid segments that are obliquely attached to the rachis. The basal leaflets are often changed into thorns.

The very flashy inflorescences have an axillary spadix and each one of them is wrapped by a spathe until their development is completed.

They are dioecious plants. The fruit is a berry that is generally elongate.

Some *Phoenix* are particularly interesting from an economic point of view because of their tasty fruit (the date is the main food of the Arabic tribes of the desert), because of their wood, and because of the milky liquid, sweet and fermentable, that is obtained from the stems and transformed into an alcoholic drink.

Cultivation. Our concern here is for their ornamental value. They are cultivated with the greatest ease, starting with the seed that is placed to germinate in a pot in a humid and warm greenhouse. Eventual pottings, using a soil formed from leaf mold, soil, and a little sand, will favor plant growth if care is taken to water abundantly.

Species and varieties. The best-known species is *Phoenix dactylifera*, the date palm, which is cultivated for its fruit. For decoration, it is surpassed by the widely used *P. canariensis*.

Cycas

Aesthetically similar to palms, even if botanically distant, and belonging to the Cycadaceae family, this genus has about 12 species, all native to lands with warm climates (China, Sonda Islands, Australia, Japan, etc.). They are cultivated as ornamental plants throughout the world, either in the greenhouse or in the ground in those regions where the climate is mild. They need the same attention as palms.

The most famous species is the *Cycas revoluta,* having a developed trunk with a crown of very large leaves that are pinnate, leathery, and dark green.

---

87. *Collinia elegans.*

89. Close up of the leaves of *Raphis.*

88, 90. The rigid, majestic elegance of the *Cycas revoluta* and a close up of the leaves in the same plant.

Succulents and cacti

Nature affirms the right to live in its simplest and most logical ways: the reduced size of Alpine plants and the various types of protection that allow this species to survive the very long winters and abundant snow storms provide an example of it. The odd-shape of orchid flowers that favors pollination by means of the pronubials is another illustration of its freakishness. The fleshy consistency of cactus plants, that allows their existence in conditions of extreme drought, is additional proof of adjustment for survival.

The terms "cactus" and "succulents" include species that are biologically and physiologically related, but are primarily descriptive of a process in which a particular adjustment to specific environmental conditions has been made. Thus it is the making of this adjustment that the species have in common and we should not be surprised to find that the plants belong to many families not even closely related botanically. (Crassulaceae, Cactaceae, Euphorbiaceae, Liliaceae, etc.).

These plants have a great importance in gardening, where they are cultivated not so much for the temporary beauty of their flowers, but mainly for the strange, but perfect and geometric architectures of their stems.

Sedum

Where there is a little soil, whether it be between two rocks that have been abandoned along a river or among the ruins of a crumbling construction or on the narrow terrace of a steep Alpine wall, in the sun and with very little water, there we find *Sedums.*

Origins. This large genus, *Sedum,* (numbering 300 species, according to some, and 150, according to others,) belongs to the *Crassulaceae* family. It is a cosmopolitan, since it is present, although in varying degrees on all continents. Many species are native to Europe, where they grow in difficult conditions.

Morphology. The *Sedums* are annual or perennial plants that are also herbaceous, and rarely suffruticose. They are fleshy, have erect or procumbent stems that can be simple or racemose and are sometimes quite matted to form a moss-like carpet. The leaves have the most various shapes and have the ability to store water; they are fleshy, succulent, globous, cylindrical, with whole or toothed margins, and they are always stipulated.

Cultivation. In the past some species of *Sedum* have attracted interest as edible plants to be consumed fresh, and as constituents of popular medicine due to their emetic and antiscorbutic properties and their effectiveness as external application on wounds. They are particularly appreciated in rock gardens or as pla[...] ings in dry corners exposed to the sun or on [...] walls or even for borders.

Their cultivation is extremely easy beca[...] *Sedums* have few demands. They are pro[...] gated easily by division of the clumps or by st[...] or root cutting. They grow on practically a[...] substrate and they need little water. The Alp[...] species and the ones of temperate climates can [...] cultivated in open ground all year around. T[...] tropical kinds need a winter shelter and can [...] cultivated in a greenhouse.

Species and varieties. About 30 s[...] cies for garden or house are known. Amo[...] them are:

Sedum alpestre, native to the Alps, has wh[...] flowers and is suitable for Alpine gardens.

S. acre, the one we call "pepper of the wall[...] is a species native to Morocco and now natur[...] ized and widely found in gardens.

S. rupestre is native to the Alps; it has num[...] ous yellow flowers.

S. Sieboldii, native to Japan, has a characteri[...] tic arrangement of the stems falling down l[...] rays and flowers in late autumn.

S. caeruleum, is a very pretty and decorati[...] little plant with small starry blue flowers.

Other species are: *S. Telphium, S. Adolphii,* [...] *praealtum,* and *S. album.*

91. *Sedum spurium* with blossoms.

9

92 93

Crassulas

Crassula is a typical genus of the Crassulaceae family that includes numerous others cultivated for the decoration of gardens and houses.

Origins. *Crassulas* have been cultivated since they were introduced in Europe from South Africa.

Morphology. They are generally erect; the leaves are simple, opposed, sessile, cone-shaped, oval or triangular, fleshy, and glabrous or pubescent or scaly. The cymose or capitate inflorescences have small white or pinkish or yellow pentamerous flowers.

Cultivation. Their cultivation does not present difficulties. In warm regions they grow in the open, while in the north they must be placed in a cold or temperate greenhouse during winter, or indoors.

They are generally propagated by cuttings in the sun, during the spring and summer months, or under glass at other times. Plant them in a soil formed from equal parts of fertile soil and clean sand, and water them sparingly during rooting.

The potting is done keeping in mind the necessity for good drainage and for a very light soil mixture without fertilizers, which may be made from three parts of sand and one part of peat to one part top soil.

Exposure to sun is important since the plants are heliophylous, or sun-loving. This applies both to those that are cultivated in the open as well as to those cultivated in the greenhouse. Watering must be light because excessive and persistent humidity is ruinous. Abundant irrigations are useful during the growing period as long as they are not too frequent and always use water with a temperature similar to that of the surrounding air. Particular care is given when repotting, if necessary in spring, and when pruning some species to make a bushy shape.

Species and varieties. The main species are:

Crassula arborescens, a plant with branches, a bare stem, and oval-elongate, dull glaucous or gray-greenish leaves and white flowers.

C. argentea, a plant which has a branched and brown stem, shiny green leaves that are oval-oblong with a short point, and flowers that bloom early (March, April).

C. falcata is a plant with a simple and non-branched stem, leaves that are sickle-shaped, opposed, and joined to the base in pairs, and abundant flowers that are red-crimson.

C. perfoliata is a plant with a simple stem, whose leaves are lanceolate, acuminate, and hollow on the upper part of the plant; the scented flowers are white.

C. lactea is a small, decorative shrub, with oval and light-green leaves; the flowers are in terminal clusters.

C. sarcocaulis is a small plant suited for rock gardens.

94

92, 93. *Crassula arborescens* with the close view of the fleshy flowers.

94. Flower of *Crassula falcata.*

Kalanchoes

The strange name of Chinese derivation refers to plants of more than 100 species that are spread not only in tropical areas, but also in South Africa, India, and South America.

Morphology. The *Kalanchoes* are herbaceous, sturdy, and shrubby plants that have an erect stem. They have opposite, fleshy, sessile, or petioled leaves. The flowers are bright with very tiny corollas which are yellow, red-purplish, or red-scarlet, appear in inflorescences shaped like a paniculated umbrella, and are tetramerous. The fruit is a capsule with four carpels.

Cultivation. *Kalanchoes* are very pretty and interesting plants whose acceptance by the public is becoming greater and greater on account of the lasting quality of the plants in houses and the long blooming period, which is possible to obtain in culture in almost all seasons. They are plants that can live in exposed locations in the open ground only in those zones where citrus growing is also possible. One must take advantage of temperate greenhouses in other areas. A moderate temperature of 60–65°F between March and September is sufficient; whereas, around 45–50°F is sufficient during the winter months.

The exposure should be to full sun and the soil mixture should be formed as already indicated for the *Crassula* genus. Always fertilize in a very small amount. Watering has to be abundant in the warm spring and summer months, must be progressively diminished after August, and then done sparingly in winter.

Since *Kalanchoes* tend to loose their leaves as they get older, pruning can be done after blooming, thus forcing the growth of new branches which will not, however, bloom as well. For this reason, the practice is not very widely spread and it is better to use a stem cutting taken between June and August. In commercial greenhouses seed propagation is currently practiced.

Species and varieties. Of more than 100 species that have been catalogued, only about 12 have commercial value and these vary in color of the flower. *Kalanchoe beharensis,* native to Madagascar, is a plant widely cultivated with great value. It grows 25 to 30 inches tall and even more, with large, triangular leaves, and yellowish-green to white flowers.

K. flammea, native to Somalia, is about 15 inches tall and has yellow and orange-scarlet flowers. *K. thyrsiflora, K. laciniata, K. marmorata, K. lanceolata, K. pinnata,* and *K. Blossfeldiana* are other very decorative species.

---

95. Young plants of *Kalanchoe pinnata.*

96. Close view of *Kalanchoe* with plantlets on the leaf margin.

97. Flowers of *Kalanchoe Blossfeldiana.*

98. Crassulaceae are recognized for the succulence of their leaves.

95

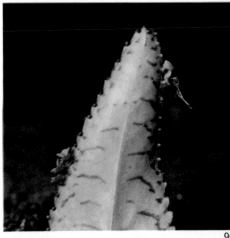
96

97

98

99 100

101

cheverias

Most species of this genus belong to the flora
Mexico and are named in honor of the Mexi-
n botanist and painter, Attanasio Echeverria.
The genus *Echeveria* belongs to the *Cras-
laceae* family and about 80 species are known,
which 20 are popular in cultivation.

Morphology. They are herbaceous plants
which have a fleshy appearance, are almost always stemless, with fat and flattened leaves arranged in thick rosettes, green-grayish in color.
The flowers are in loose racemes or in spikes
in paniculated umbels and have a pentamerous base. The corolla is angular with 5 corners,
yellow, orange or pink.

Cultivation. *Echeverias* are cultivated as
house plants, but it is in the garden that they find
their prominence. They can be used successfully
rocky locations or in small groups as a border.
they are put close to stones, they are particu-
ly suited for bedding. They are also suited for
right designs in sphagnum where they can be
constructed as columns and used together with
gonias and other colored leaf plants.
They are cultivated all year around in warmer
areas, where the temperature never drops to

freezing. In cool areas they must spend the winter under a shelter, in a greenhouse, or indoors.
They are propagated by leaf cuttings or by sepa-
rating the basal shoots.

Species and varieties. The most popular species are:
Echeveria glauca is caulous, with rosettes of
2½ to 4 inches and leaves which are powdery
grayish-green sometimes showing pinkish
shades. The flowers are red and bloom in spring
or fall.
E. setosa is covered with white hairs from
which its name is derived. The rosettes are almost globular; the red flowers bloom in July to
August.
E. multicaulis has a hairy and greatly
branched stem; the rosettes are large and loose
with green leaves; the flowers are red with a
winter blooming in warm places.
E. elegans and *E. agavoides* are also species
with ornamental value.

---

99. Flower beds bounded by *Echeverias*.

100. *Echeveria elegans* in cultivation.

101. The rosette shape of the *Echeveria*.

Aloe

This is a typical genus of the South African countryside and has climatically adjusted to tropical regions especially along the coast. The long red and yellow tufts of its inflorescence and the characteristic acuminate leaves complement the sea.

Origins. The genus *Aloe* belongs to the Liliaceae family, which includes numerous plants of interest to gardeners. *Aloe* include about 180 species native to Southern Africa, Madagascar, Arabia, India, Canary Islands, and South Western Mediterranean regions, and all have interesting flowers and ornamental foliage.

Morphology. Characteristic of the *Aloe* is the large variety of forms that is offered by their species. They are either stemless plants with more or less large basal leaves or they are tree-like plants with dichotomous branching. They have fleshy, thin leaves which are triangular in shape, more or less toothed, and sword-shaped or spiny on the margins and sometimes all over the surface. They are produced at the top of the stalk or arranged in a basal rosette.

The numerous flowers are in racemes or spikes on a long scape; they are brightly colored in red or yellow and are often striped in pale shades. The fruit is a trivalved capsule containing numerous flattened and winged seeds.

The genus *Aloe* has important scientific and economic interest. The *Aloes* not only have ornamental use, but are also in the official Pharmacopoeia as laxatives and eupeptics both in human and veterinary medicine. From the *Aloe* (*A. perfoliata*) come the fibers for bulky fabric which have a local value, especially in India.

Cultivation. The *Aloe* species for garden are of great interest because, to a greater or smaller degree, they are all ornamental. They are cultivated in full sun in warm climates and in greenhouses elsewhere. Their shapes, plastic-like and with a morbid rigidity, match well even with modern architecture. Species of a smaller size are useful in the decoration of apartments.

For cultivation outdoors, sunny locations are necessary, remembering to allow space for full development when planting outdoors.

They are grown in a temperate greenhouse (4 to 50°F). They prefer a soil mixture that is sandy and well drained. The use of small, shallow pots with a soil mix of leaf mold and top soil is suggested.

They should be moderately watered especially in winter; while in the greenhouse they require much light and a dry atmosphere. Transplanting is only done when plants become pot-bound.

Propagation takes place by division of the clumps, by offshoots or by cuttings. They can also be reproduced by seed at the end of winter in a hothouse.

Species and varieties. The most important ornamental species are briefly described. *Aloe africana,* native to South Africa, is tree-like and may reach 10 feet in height. It is very popular in southern gardens and blooms in summer.

A. ciliaris comes from Southern Africa; it a viny species that lives in the open and blooms all year in Southern California.

104

Haworthia

A. ferox is from South Africa; leaves are
ouped into thick rosettes having a glaucous
olor; the thorns are reddish-brown and the
owers are orange.

A. humilis, of African origin, is a very pretty
ecies in numerous varieties and hybrids. *A.
umilis* var. *echinata* and *A. arborescens* var.
achythyrsa* are worthy of mention for their
rge inflorescences.

A. vera from the Mediterranean region is well
djusted to the South. Other popular types in-
lude: *A. striata, A. variegata,* and *A. bravi-
olia.*

02. Cactus greenhouse; in the foreground, an *Aloe.*

03. Inflorescence of *Aloe.*

04. *Haworthia fasciata* with leaves, elegantly deco-
rated by white tubercles.

This genus bears the name of the English
botanist A. H. Haworth, who was a great
scholar on cactus. The plants are native to South
Africa. *Haworthia* belongs to the Liliaceae family and includes about 60 species.

Morphology. These succulents are perennial, small-sized, stemless plants. The leaves are
thick, fleshy, pointed or truncated; they are often
covered with white and even transparent tubercles. They are arranged in the stipes in over-
lapped rows or arranged in basal rosettes.

The flowers are white, green, or striped with
red, are arranged in simple or panicled racemes,
and have a tubular shape. The fruit is a capsule
with three valves containing compressed and angular seeds.

Cultivation. *Haworthias* are plants of ornamental interest and are particularly suited as

house plants. They are easy to cultivate; their
culture must take place in full sun only in the
best location of warm areas. In the cool zones
they should be protected in greenhouses or hot
beds in winter.

Propagation is easily accomplished by vegetative means using root shoots or cuttings. Reproduction by seeds is easy, but produces plants
quite variable and unlike the parent plant.

Species and varieties. The most important species are:

Haworthia fasciata has rigid, leathery leaves
that are sharp and have regular stripes given by
white formations of tubercles.

H. margaritifera has very sharp leaves covered with large white tubercles.

H. margaritifera var. *granata* has more
crowded tubercles.

H. retusa has rather soft leaves which are
rough on the back and truncate.

Mesembryanthemum

Single daisies, Korean chrysanthemums, fig marigolds, or small gerberas. The nomenclature of *Mesembryanthemum* is very confusing.

Mesembryanthemum is a genus of the Aizoaceae family encompassing over 1,000 species.

Origins.
They have a tropical origin and most of them come from South Africa. Some grow in rocky areas, others on sandy soils. Some are found near the sea. All are native to semi-arid tropics and subtropics.

Morphology.
They are succulent, mostly herbaceous plants, sometimes tree-like and sometimes even without a stem, an extreme expression of a very advanced condition of xerophytism. They have fleshy, conical or pyramidial triangular leaves that are green or even glaucous, bluish or purple.

The flashy and very bright flowers are abundantly produced in different colors: white, yellow, and in all shades of red and pink to purple and orange. They have long and narrow petals that are very graceful and open up in the daylight only by the direct action of the sun. The fruit is a capsule with a mechanical opening and closing of its valves in conditions of humidity. There is the exception of the *Carpobrotus edulis* and *C. acinaciformis* in which the fruit is fleshy and edible and is consumed by some African people; from this the plant receives its common name "Hottentot-Fig."

A certain interest has developed from the fact that some species have edible leaves, even though the Mesembryanthemums are s mainly used as ornamental plants for the garc more than for the house.

Cultivation.
In the south they may be c tivated in the open. In the north these pla must be protected during winter. They need s and dry, sandy soil, low in organic matter.

Propagation by seeds is done in April ir greenhouse where they are sowed in sand wh the humidity is increased. They are easily prof gated by cuttings and by division.

Species and varieties.
The most markable species of Mesembryanthemums a

Corpobrotus acinaciformis, from Sou Africa but now naturalized in some countries produces beautiful pink-purple flowers.

Carpobrotus edulis, similar to *C. acinacif mis,* but with yellow or violet flowers and tria gular leaves, has escaped and grows wild southern California.

Cryophytum crystallinum, Ice Plant (s called because of the presence on their ligh green leaves of crystalline droplets), has brig chromatic effects; the flowers are white or pin

Dorotheanthus Bellidiformis is a very beau ful species, appreciated for the abundant bloo ing with a palette of colors.

Lampranthus roseus is sometimes found cc ering slopes with a compact carpet that is sca tered with bright pink flowers.

105

106

105-108. Palette of colors in the flowers of *Mese bryanthemum* and related genera.

107

108

Opuntias

This genus is native to the Western Hemisphere from Canada to the Straits of Magellan. Over 250 species are described. They are known by the common names Prickly-Pear, Tuna, or Cholla.

Morphology.
Genus *Opuntia* belongs to the family of the Cactaceae and has plants of variable sizes and shapes which display erect to prostrate habits and range from small to tall, even reaching the appearance of shrubs up to 15 to 20 feet. They have fibrous or thickened roots. The stems and the branches are formed by many smaller ones so that they look like large and fleshy leaves attached to one another. The actual leaves, instead, are small and drop early. On the sides of the stem numerous thorns are borne that can be solitary or in groups, bare or characteristically covered and accompanied by fuzzy bristles. Some species are thornless.

The flowers grow on the distal parts of the areoles, and have green sepals or a color which is very close to that of the petals, usually a flashy green, yellow or red. The fruit is a fleshy globous berry that can be ellipsoidal or ovoidal, spiny or spineless, with many seeds buried in the pulp.

Cultivation.
Some species of *Opuntia* are cultivated in warm areas in full sun to obtain the edible fruits. Others are cultivated for decorative purposes. Wherever the climate is cold, th need the greenhouse. They need well-drain soil that is slightly alkaline.

They can very easily be propagated becau from every section that is detached from t stem, one can obtain a new plant. Waterin should not be too frequent or too abundant; th need much light and full sun.

Species and varieties.
Among t most interesting species are: *Opuntia vulgaris* native to South America, has a modest size, wi yellow flowers and edible fruit. It is used as u derstock for grafting of more delicate species

O. Cylindrica comes from Ecuador and Per It is a very decorative plant on account of i stem that has cylindrical sections and its scarl flower. It is used as understock for grafting.

O. Ficus indica is the famous Indian l widely spread in all warm regions.

O. diademata presents odd pimples on the le sections.

O. elata, O. leucotricha, and *O. microdas* are other ornamental species.

109. *Opuntia tunicata,* showing strong spines.

110. *Pountia Bigelowii.*

111-114. Close-up of fruits and flowers of *Opun* species.

109

110

111

112

113

114

116

115   117

Cereus

Plants with stylized and elegant forms, that have the shapes of modern architecture, *Cereus* are a distinctive feature of the sunny countryside of Central and South America and of the islands of the West Indies.

The genus *Cereus* belongs to the *Cactaceae* family and includes about 30 species, some of them having an interesting ornamental appearance. Many plants are called "Cereus" while they really belong to related genera such as *(Acanthocereus, Selenicereus, Echinopsis, etc.)*

Morphology.   These are perennial, succulent plants that have a slender appearance (some of them look like gigantic candelabra). The stalks are furrowed by ribs whose number varies from 4 to 9; they can be more or less branched and are always without leaves.

The large showy flowers appear along the ribs and have a tubular receptacle that can be green or dark lead-green, glabrous or hairy; the numerous petals are in bright colors. Each blossom lasts only one night. The fruit is a fleshy berry that often is edible, and contains numerous small black seeds.

Cultivation.   *Cereus* are cultivated for ornamental purposes outdoors in frost-free areas. In the northern areas the *Cereus* need a winter shelter and when they are young, they are appreciated as a plant for the house.

Their culture follows the direction already given for the other cacti. They need a soil that has little organic matter and is always well drained so that injury from excess water is avoided. Propagation is by seeds or by cuttings. *Cereus* are excellent understocks in grafting more delicate *Cactaceae*.

Species and varieties.   The most popular species are: *Cereus peruvianus*, which good in coastal gardens and grows to 40 feet. very interesting variety of it is *C. peruvianu* var. *monstruosus* that has a warty, irregularly crested stem.

C. azureus grows to 3 or 4 feet, has a thin ste that is branched from the base, and has a bluis green color when it is young and a dark gree color when it becomes older.

---

115. Greenhouse of Cactus plants with echinoca and *Cereus*.

116. The odd shape of the *Cereus variabilis*.

117. *Cactaceae* remind us of thorns and an arid c mate.

119

118

Cephalocereus (Old man cactus)

This genus includes species with the stem covered by little areoles with spines that are mixed with long whiskers and with a terminal tuft that is larger and makes the adult plants look like a cartoon of an old man's head.

Origins. The *Cephalocereus* genus belongs to the Cactaceae family and includes about 20 species that are native to the southern United States to Ecuador, and to Brazil.

Morphology. They are plants with a columnar stem that can be simple or branched, ribbed or spreading, and with long bristles.

The flowers are numerous and variously colored according to the species. The fruits are globular, small berries.

Cultivation. The culture is not difficult and is the same as for other Cactaceae; the only concern must be given to the temperature which must always be above 50°F.

Species and varieties. The most commonly cultivated species are: *Cephalocereus senilis,* which is better known by the name of "Old Man Cactus"; and *C. languinosus, C. Royenii,* and *C. Russelianus.*

---

118. The attractive bloom of the Cactaceae is a reward for the short duration of the flowers.

119. *Cephalocereus senilis.*

120. *Cephalocereus senilis* in company with other cacti.

120

12

123

124

Mamillarias

These are outstanding plants because of the perfect symmetry of their shape that makes them fine house plants.

Origins. Most species are native to Mexico and Central America.

The *Mamillaria* genus belongs to the Cactaceae family and numbers over 200 species.

Morphology. *Mamillarias* are small sized plants having a spherical or cylindrical shape. The stems bear many protuberances that look like tubercles or Mammilia and are arranged in spirals which present at the top a small tomentose areole that bears thorns set as a halo of rays. The thorns are interesting for their varied shape and for their range in color from black to white and from yellow to red.

The flowers are white, red, or yellow; they are small and are shaped like short bells arranged like a crown that is usually turned toward the top of the branch. The fruits are small berries that are red, white, or rose; they are very attractive and often a crown of fruits accompanies a crown of flowers emphasizing the ornamental value of the plant.

Cultivation. These plants are not difficult to grow; they are much in demand as a decoration both in the exotic rock garden, where they show their beauty, and in the house. They are easily propagated by basal offshoots that grow as a new plant. One must remember that the *Mamillarias* develop well in large shallow pots and are particularly appreciated if they are in a large colony.

They do not have particular demands as far a soil is concerned, even if almost all species lik the presence of lime. A suitable mixture can b formed by garden mold, well-decomposed lea mold, and river sand in equal amounts with th addition of lime. Good drainage, little wate and much sun will ensure success.

Species and varieties. We call atten tion to the following species:

Mamillaria spinosissima, of Mexican origi has a cylindrical shape, lead-colored leaves, an red flowers.

M. microcarpa, native to Texas and Arizon is globose or cylindrical and branched at th base with purplish-red flowers.

M. prolifera (=M. pusilla) is very commo and is appreciated for the high decorative valu it has a spheroidal or ovoid shape and is matte with reddish or yellowish thorns. It has yello flowers.

M. arida, of California origin, is a rounde plant that has conical tubercles and yellowis thorns shaped like rays and yellow flowers.

---

121. Specimen of *Mamillaria fragilis* that looks li a mysterious "totem pole."

122. Here is an example of how the peculiar artist of Nature covers up the big leafless stems of t Cactaceae with geometrically arranged thorn

123-124. *Mamillaria tringularis* and detail of areol bearing thorns.

126-

125   127

chinocactus

These are the cacti that draw the most atten-
n from vicitors to exotic gardens, because of
eir shape and their generally large dimensions.

rigins.   The plants of this genus belong to
e Cactaceae family and are native to southwest
S. and Mexico. As is the case of other genera
Cactaceae, taxonomic controversies abound.
e species that are attributed to it vary, accord-
g to authors, from about 1,000 species to only
 species, and include some species with very
y flowers.

lorphology.   The plants are globose or
lindrical; they are leafless, depressed at the
ex, with very evident mostly vertical ribs that
e covered with strong straight thorns.

The flowers are arranged at the top; they are
all or large, mostly yellow or shades of yel-
w; they open up in full sun and persist longer
an for other Cactaceae.

ultivation.   Interest in these plants is ex-
usively for their ornamental value and they are
ltivated both for the garden, in the open in
ost-free areas, and as house plants. Propaga-
n takes place by seeds, because the *Echicactus*
 not produce basal shoots.

They are very demanding as far as heat is
ncerned, but they enjoy semi-sunny locations.
ey also require abundant watering during the
mmer, especially in the warmer hours of the
y. A suitable substratum is formed by mixing
o parts of course sand and one part of peat-
oss with one part wood duff and one part loam.

Species and varieties.   *Echinocactus
Grusonii,* has a globous shape and large dimensions; its thorns are grouped in fours, are somewhat transparent, and sulphur yellow; the
flowers are yellow.

E. horizonthalonius, with modest dimensions, is globose or short-cylindrical when mature, with brown or reddish thorns.

E. ingens, grows to 5 feet high and 4 feet in
diameter, with brown spines and yellow flowers.

---

125. *Echinocactus Grusonii* and *Euphorbia.*
126-127.   Symmetrical structure of *Echinocactus*
    with flowers arranged on top.
128-130.   Close up of a *Echinocactus* in bloom.

129

130

131

Epiphyllum

This is a group of cacti that both in appearance and in cultural requirements depart from the groups previously described. Furthermore they have a familiar appearance because they are commonly cultivated along with related genera, such as *Zygocactus, Schlumbergera,* etc.

Origins. They are epiphtic plants and live in tropical forests of Central America. They belong to the Cactaceae family and they are succulent, bushy plants which have flattened branches with stalks that look like long crenate or toothed leaves.

Their very pretty flowers are large, white, red, pink or yellow, very numerous and arranged around the margins of the stems. The fruits, of an elongated shape, are red and contain many black seeds.

Cultivation. Cultivation is not difficult. They need shady locations and abundant waterings during the summer. They can live outdoors in the warm weather, but in winter they need to be taken indoors where only the minimum amount of water should be applied.

Contrary to other cacti, they need a soil rich in organic matter which can be a mixture of peat, rotted manure, leaf mold, and loam in equal amounts with the addition of a little sand. Propagation can be by seed or by cuttings. A curiosity is the grafting on to *Pereskia aculeata,* to form little trees having an ornamental effect.

Species and varieties. Among the most important species are: *Epiphyllum Ackermannii,* with white and crimson flowers, and *E. oxypetalum* with pink and white, scented petals. There are numerous attractive hybrids.

---

131. One of the cacti that are widely grown: *Schlumbergera,* related to the *Epiphyllum.*

132. Flower of *Epiphyllum.*

132

Flowering plants

nthurium

Originating in the tropical and subtropical re-
ns of Central America, the genus belongs to
Araceae family, and has numerous species
ich are perennials, with erect or climbing
ms. The leaves are entire, lobate or divided
d have an oval, cordate, arrow-like or spear-
e shape; they are green or often in metallic
des and almost always have long stalks.
The inflorescence is an upright, wrapped or
nkled spadix with a large, green, yellow, red
purple spathe. The fruit is a berry.

ultivation. Demanding constant atten-
n, they are plants for warm, humid green-
uses at day temperatures of from 70 to 75°F
d from 65 to 70°F at night. They require
fused light for which it is necessary to shade
greenhouse. The creeping species need sup-
rts such as a stake lined with sphagnum or
munda fiber.

Anthuriums are grown in a light, porous mix-
re that is formed of chopped sphagnum, tiny
eces of osmunda roots, top soil in equal
ounts, plus sand. Some advise the addition of
arcoal in the case of Anthuriums for flowers,
the composition of a rather clayey soil for the
liage varieties. It is essential to drain the pot
refully and place the plants so that the crown
ll be slightly below the top edge of the pot,
ling up the space that remains with sphagnum.
his favors the development of advantitious
ots that develop in the axil of the leaves after
e plants bloom.

Abundant watering during the vegetative period and frequent liquid fertilization is given.
The annual repotting is dependent on the
growth and vigor of the plant.

Anthuriums propagate by seeds that are sown
shortly after picking; otherwise they lose their
viability. Seeding is done in late summer or fall
in well-drained containers filled with leaf mold
and sphagnum.

They are also propagated by cuttings in June
to July, using all the stem, including the part
underground; layering can also be used or the
clumps can be divided.

Species and varieties. Certain kinds
are grown for flowers and others for leaves.
Among the Anthuriums for flowers are A. Andreanum, which also has a pretty foliage, and
A. Scherzerianum (Flamingo flower); both have
numerous hybrids.

Among the foliage Anthuriums are A. crystallinum, with very large leaves that are velvety
green with light veins, and A. Veitchii, with
huge, metallic green leaves that are darker when
the plant is mature.

Among creeping species are A. miquelianum
and A. Kalbreyeri.

133. Spathe and inflorescence of Anthurium Scherzerianum.

134-137. Spathes and inflorescences of Anthurium
Andreanum.

138. Cultivation of Anthurium in the greenhouse.

135

136

137

38

Callas

After many taxonomic changes, the genus *Calla* has been given the name of *Zantadeschia* in honor of the Italian botanist Francesco Zantedeschi; the old name calla has become the common name.

Calla, whose inflorescence looks like an extraordinary shell, has a proud snobbish appearance whenever it is seen alone, but, once it is put close to other exotic plants, especially outdoors, along water streams, or around the edges of ponds, it acquires all the warm flashy splendor that is so undeniably African in flavor.

Origins. The *Zantadeschia* genus belongs to the Araceae family. Membership includes 8 species which are native to Southern Africa and have been cultivated for ornamental purposes for several centuries.

Morphology. They are perennial ornamental plants that are typical of humid, swampy areas; they have a large rhizome from which the leaves arise on a long, spongy stalk. The leaf is large, arrowhead-shaped, lanceolate, or heart shaped with a wavy border; its color is a uniform green or spotted with white or yellow.

The spadix inflorescence includes a white, yellow, or rose spathe, A-shaped and rounded at the base, terminating in a point that is curved downwards; the inflorescence is carried by an erect peduncle that is as long as, or a little longer than, the leaves. The fruit is a berry.

Cultivation. Callas are cultivated as pot-plants or in open ground during the warm weather, or as cut flowers.

Propagation is by seeds, sown immediately after maturation, but more often propagation is by division of the rhizomes. The rhizomes themselves are planted in large pots filled with a mixture rich in humus.

It is important to provide these plants with a period of rest after blooming which can be initiated by diminishing the frequency of waterings.

Planted outdoors in the spring, the calla flowers in June to September. After blooming, the plant is allowed to become dry by fewer waterings. The rhizomes are then taken out of the ground and placed in pots that are full of sand in order to prevent them from drying out. They are replanted in the spring.

1

Species and varieties. The best-known calla is the *Zantedeschia aethiopica* of which there are several varieties: *minor,* 12 to 15 inches tall; *devoniensis,* that is scented; *candidissima; grandiflora;* and *gigantea,* with a beautiful effect because of the shape and color of the spathe.

Z. albo-maculata has acuminate and white-spotted leaves.

Z. melanoleuca has oval lanceolate leaves that are spotted with white and a spathe with a purple spot at the base.

Worthy of mention are the *Z. Elliottian* with a yellow spathe, and *Z. Rehmanni,* with pink spathe having wild shades.

---

139. A magnificent plant of blooming Calla.

140. Young sprout of *Zantedeschi Elliottiana.*

141,142. Calla: a close-up of the spathe.

Euphorbias

This is a very large group of plants all native of tropical, subtropical, and temperate regions of the world, where many of them have been known since antiquity because of their medicinal properties.

All the *Euphorbias* secrete a whitish caustic latex that is in some species extremely poisonous. Some species are weeds in gardens, lawns, and pastures. About 100 are considered ornamental.

Morphology. Belonging to the Euphorbiaceae family, the *Euphorbia* genus is variable, including herbaceous annuals, perennials, shrubby and tree-like arboreal plants, and large-leaved and Cactus-like plants.

Characteristic is the structure of the cup-shaped inflorescence that is formed by a peduncled female flower surrounded by many male monostamened flowers and that is emphasized by leaf bracts which are more or less developed and greenish or brightly colored.

Cultivation. The species of the *Euphorbia* genus that are of concern here are those cultivated for cutting flowers or for pot plants. Our attention is directed to *E. pulcherrima*, commonly called *poinsettia*, the popular Christmas flower which, together with *F. fulgens* and *F. splendens*, are the most famous and most cultivated.

Because of their various forms, *Euphorbias* have different demands and consequently different techniques of cultivation from species to species. The culture of the first-mentioned species can be done outdoors only in frost-free locations. Propagation is by cuttings. It is good to immerse the cuttings in water for a few hours to eliminate the coagulated latex from the cut. The soil must be a good top soil, with the addition of organic matter. In their vegetative period, frequent watering and liquid fertilizations are required.

Euphorbia fulgens has similar requirements whereas *E. splendens* is grown as described for succulents.

Species and varieties. *Euphorbia pulcherrima* (Poinsettia) is a magnificent shrubby plant that attracts our attention for the bright color of its large red-scarlet bracts. It blooms from December to March. Also the varieties: *alba, rosea, plenissima.*

E. fulgens is cultivated because of its numerous flowers that are carried by elegant racemes.

E. splendens is very common and noted for its spiny stems.

Other interesting *Euphorbias* are the *F. abyssinica,* the *F. resinifera,* the *F. tridentata* that have the requirements of the Cactaceae.

143. *Euphorbia splendens.*

144. Spiny branch and inflorescence of *Euphorbia splendens.*

145. The classical and widely-spread inflorescence of the *Euphorbia pulcherrima,* the very popular Christmas flower.

146. *Euphorbia resinifera.*

147

148

Saintpaulia

Like the last born in a large family who dra
attentions, so the *Saintpaulia*, that has arriv
from the Kilimanjaro mountains around the e
of last century, has been greeted by admirati
and favor.

Morphology. Known as the African v
let, the *Saintpaulia* genus belongs to the G
neriaceae family and has 20 species, of which t
most typical is *S. ionantha.*

The plants are small, perennial, and herb
ceous; they grow to about 6 inches in heigl
They have leaves that are oval, with a flesl
petiole, dark green, hairy, and arranged in
rosette.

The flowers, on a cymose inflorescence, ha
a monopetalous corolla that is irregular, has
lobes, and is largely campanulate. The color
the flowers ranges from white and pink to purp
with bright yellow stamens. The fruit is
oblong capsule with small ellipsoidial seeds.

Cultivation. The interest in this pretty l
tle plant is justified by the dainty beauty of
leaves and flowers, by the long duration
blooming, by the tolerance to indoor condition
by the possibility, during the summer, of placi
it in a shady position in the garden to for
stupendous spots of color.

The *Saintpaulia* reproduces well by leaf cu
tings to be taken at any season of the year. Th
are placed in peat and sand at a temperature
75 to 80°F. Eventually they are potted in a lig
mixture of leaf mold, peat, soil and sand. Bloor
ing takes place for most of the year, but partic
larly throughout the summer.

During its vegetative period it has to be w
tered normally, being careful not to wet tl
leaves that are very delicate. The plants a
grown at 70 to 75°F in diffused light. During tl
rest period, they should be kept at 55 to 60°
and little water given.

Species and varieties. The best-know
species of this genus is *S. ionantha,* that we ha
already mentioned, of which, varieties wil
white as well as pink and violet, flowers a
known. The flowers can be simple or doub
flowers, and the leaves are variegated.

147-150. The African violet, botanically known b
the name of *Saintpaulia ionantha,* has varieti
with violet, pink, and white flowers, either sing
or double.

149

15

151

152

oya

This plant attracts attention because of its almost artificial looking flowers and attractive foliage.

origins. The *Hoya* genus belongs to the Asclepiadaceae family and has about 70 species, all native to the Far East. A few of them are cultivated in greenhouses or as a house plant.

Morphology. *Hoyas* are plants having usually a climbing or creeping habit, with persistent leaves that are oval-shaped and of a leathery consistency.

The single, small, starred flowers with a lightly colored center are arranged in compact, axillary, umbrella-shaped inflorescences; characteristic is the waxy appearance of the corollas and their delicate fragrance. The fruits are follicles containing seeds with a pappus.

Cultivation. Interesting, even if little-known at present, they are cultivated for the beauty of the flowers and are very successful as house plants, where, if taken care of, they last well.

They are propagated by cuttings, or by layering their long stems. They grow best in a light textured soil that is rich in organic matter, made three parts organic matter, one part top soil,

and one-half part sand. The soil must be well drained. They grow best in light shade; blossoming occurs in summer.

Usually grown in pots, they can be used in gardens in the summer and trained on a trellis.

Species and varieties. Among the best-known species is *Hoya carnosa* (wax plant), undoubtedly the most popular species for its "wax flowers" that are white with a rose center and are very delicately scented. Varieties include *variegata* and *exotica,* and cultivar "Silver Pink."

H. imperialis, with large, brown-purple flowers having a creamy white crown, is more demanding than *Hoya carnosa* because it requires a warmer temperature.

H. bella is a bushy, more dwarf species. Other species are *H. globulosa, H. multiflora,* and *H. bandaensis.*

151-152. *Hoya carnosa* is an exotic looking plant whose flowers are often called wax flowers.

153

154

156

157

Pelargonium

These plants have red, pink, white, and multicolored flowers. They are easily grown in boxes on a balcony, either individually or as a mass planting in a garden, in a pot on the window sill, or in an ornamental jar on the patio. They can be grown in any sunny location and will flower reliably.

Geranium is the common name, but botanically, they belong to the genus *Pelargonium,* of the Geraniaceae family (the *Geranium* genus includes native and cultivated species that have minor importance as garden plants). The scientific name *Pelargonium* derives from the Greek and means "stork," in the same way that Geranium means "crane" because of the likeness of the seeds of these plants to the long beaks of these long-legged birds.

Origins.
It is a very large genus with many natural species, but today we grow hybrids and improved cultivars; there are many available and the number is increasing through hybridization.

The first species of *Pelargonium* introduced in Europe came from the Colony of the Cape, and was probably the *P. zonale.*

Morphology.
Pelargoniums are perennial, shrubby plants, with herbaceous or woody, erect or procumbent stems. Their leaves have different shapes according to the species or to the varieties; they can be opposed or alternate, simple or compound, lobate or entire or indented.

The flowers are irregular and are axillary, peduncled, and in umbels; the calyx has 5 sepals, the corolla has 5 petals with all the shades of the red, from pink to dark violet; in addition, white and sometimes yellow appear in them. The very long fruit is pentacarpellary and dehiscent.

Cultivation.
The cultivation of the geranium is not difficult even if its great popularity is more a demonstration of tolerance than of care. Its propagation is by seeds or by cuttings. Reproduction by seed is mainly used in the development of new cultivars.

The cuttings can be taken in spring or fall, but the optimum time varies with the location and method of growing. Once the cuttings have rooted, they are placed in pots and, in the case of large flowered geraniums, they are topped—leaving three buds that will favor the development of three branches.

Species and varieties.
Pelargonium zonale is the most common geranium; it has a busy appearance and an erect growth habit. In favorable conditions it can form shrubs that can even reach 6 feet in height. The typical species is very rare, since the culture is today dominated by many cultivars that are derived from crossing the *P. zonale* with the *P. inquinans.*

We can separate the geraniums according to the colors of the leaves into varieties with silve three-colored, lead-colored leaves, etc. Ti zonal pelargoniums can also be distinguished their dwarf varieties.

P. peltatum is the classical ivy geranium th is suitable for decorating porches, terraces, wa and is used in hanging baskets. Its varieties a numerous.

P. domesticum is famous with the commo name of "Martha Washington Geranium." It a very pretty plant and is cultivated today many varieties; it flowers only once a year.

Numerous geraniums have scented leaves ar the range of their scents is great. They belong many species among which are *P. odorat. simum, P. crispum, P. graveolens.*

---

153. The classical and traditional geranium is t Pelargonium zonale.

154. Cutting of *Pelargonium zonale.*

155. Cutting of ivy-leafed geranium *(Pelargoniu peltatum).*

156. The delicate flower of the "Martha Washingto Geranium," botanically Pelargonium dome ticum.

157, 158. Two cultivars of *Pelargonium.*

159

160

161

162

hododendrons and Azaleas

We have again a conflict in the terminology.
e call them Azaleas but botanically, they be-
ng to the rhododendrons.

rigins. The genus *Rhododendron* belongs
the Ericaceae family and has so many species
at a discord exists concerning their number. It
native to a wide area including China, Korea,
pan, and other Asiatic zones, and to several
nes in Europe and North America.

orphology. Rhododendrons are shrubs
even small trees. They have alternate leaves
at often are close together at the top of the
anches; they are entire, leathery, deciduous or
rsistent.
Their large and flashy flowers have many col-
s: white, pink, red, violet, yellow; they can be
litary or more often grouped into corymbs.
e calyx has 5 sepals and an irregular corolla
at is funnel-shaped, tubular, bell-shaped, sub-
unded. The fruit is an oblong or shortened
psule.

ultivation. A great interest is offered by
namental species and varieties for garden or
cultivation in the greenhouse. The nature of
r topic does not allow us to go in the descrip-
n of rhododendrons for all uses. Instead, we
l briefly deal with the forcing of types suitable
potted plants.

The material from which we start is botanically very heterogeneous and results from much
hybridization. Such material is grouped into sections according to the technical-morphological
characteristics. *Rhododendron indicum, R.
Kaempferi, R. molle, R. simsii,* and *R. obtusum*
are all species used in developing our present day
types.

Azaleas require an acid soil with a pH of 4.0
to 5.0. Peat is excellent to use. Perfect drainage
is required.

Cuttings are taken in July and August from
outdoor plants or in the spring after flowering of
the plants that were grown in the greenhouse.

They may require 2 to 3 years to become large
flowering sized plants.

In their second year they are placed outdoors
and periodically pruned to develop an attractive
plant. During all the period of cultivation, azaleas demand a great deal of water.

Forcing is done from Christmas to Easter,
after allowing a dormant period of from 6 to 8
weeks.

159-163. The azaleas, botanically *Rhododendrons,*
with their beautiful flashy flowers of different colors and long duration.

163

Orchids

The Orchidaceae *family has more than 500 genera and includes more than 20,000 species.*

The name derives from one of the genera: Orchis. *According to Mythology, Orchis was a young man who tried to approach a priestess of Bacchus; he was discovered and therefore the god had him killed by wild animals and later transformed into an orchid flower.*

The family of Orchidaceae *is widely spread all over the world, with terrestrial plants in temperate and cold climates and epiphytic plants in tropical climates.*

In the second half of 1800, a new era for the cultivation of orchids began with the production of the first interspecific and intergeneric hybrids that are now common. Today the cultivation of orchids continues to supply an active market and to generate the same degree of enthusiasm that was characteristic of the pioneers. A great value of these plants is the very pretty and bizarre shape of the flower, the enchanting color and the long keeping quality.

Because of the large number of genera, because of their very different shapes and the varied environment in which they live, it is impossible to proceed to a description on the species level. We will give a few comments concerning the vegetative organs and the flowers.

Roots. *We distinguish normal roots from aerial. The normal roots are similar to those of other plants, but they are characterized by the presence of a mycorrhiza symbiosis that is present with the first stages of development of the seed and without which, in nature, the young plants cannot take roots.*

The aerial roots are useful instead, for absorbing water, both as a liquid and from humid air; if they have chlorophyll, they take on an assimilatory function and sometimes also a support function.

Root tubercles. *There is another transformation of the roots frequently found in Orchidaceae and is the result of the apparent growing together of numerous, simple roots. Their function is to store reserve substances.*

Stems, rhizomes, pseudobulbs. *Orchid stems can be monopodial (the main axis develops more than the lateral ones) or sympodial (the lateral axis overtakes the main one).*

Other special formations are the pseudobulbs, organs with different shape and dimensions, but more commonly ovoidal. They are tuberized stems and have a reserve function. Solitary or grouped, the leaves are present at the time of the pseudobulb in various numbers depending on the species.

Leaves. *Leaves vary in shape, width, and color are generally sessile, single, and persistent. In many species the dark green color is absent and the leaf appears glaucous, marbled, dotted, and variegated. Except for very rare cases, the leaves do not offer any ornamental interest.*

Flowers, inflorescence. *Bizarre and stupendous, they have the strangest shapes, but in any case they always look original and very elegant, even though they sometimes appear monstruous and cold. Their structure is complicated and it is the result of transformations in function suitable for insect pollination such as pronubial insects. On the larger types, pollination is in a few cases by birds.*

The flowers can be solitary (Cypripedium) or in axillary, terminal or basal inflorescences. The male organs grow together with the female and are often transformed into petaloid organs called staminodes.

The most developed petal is called the lip or labellum and takes on different shapes. The ovary is inferior, tricarpellary and is twisted into a spiral.

The cultivation of orchids is not easy. It is necessary for each species to be grown under conditions simulating their native environment as far as the growing medium and the climate (temperature, humidity, light, ventilation) are concerned, although they are tolerant plants. The technique differs whether one wants to cultivate terrestrial or epiphytic orchids.

Greenhouse temperatures may be hot, temperate, or cold; growing substratum may be sphagnum, roots of osmunda fern, fir bark, peat, or sand or a mixture of these.

Reproduction by seeds, once the symbiotic function of the mycorrhizia endotrophic fungus, is not facilitated by nutrient cultures of agar-agar or gelatine, and is strictly for experts.

A tuberoid body, called a protocorm, develops from the seed in about two months, from which, in 12 to 18 months from the time of sowing, a little plant with the first leaves will develop.

The first blooming will take place, according to the species, from 5 to 12 years later, but the long wait is compensated for by the beauty and value of the flower and by the long duration of the plant.

Orchids multiply by: the fractioning of the rhizome, ensuring to the new plant at least two pseudobulbs; by division of the shoots; and by fragments of the stem provided with roots.

16

16

1

elias

aelia is considered as one of the most beauti-
and appreciated genus in the Orchidaceae
ily and it includes about 40 species and an
efinite number of hybrids that are both inter-
:ific and intergeneric.

orphology. *Laelia* flowers are large and
hy, single or in terminal racemes, and are
erally scented. They have subequal, lanceo-
, both free and united sepals; the petals are
ger and larger, generally plain, with a more
less distinctive trilobous labellum. The colors
very delicate.

ıltivation. They are grown in the green-
use with a mild temperature (never below
'F at night during the winter) with a high
midity. Watering must be frequent, even more
quent in spring (about every two days), and
n less frequent after blooming during their
riod of rest. Water having the same tempera-
e as the air is always used. Sprinklings of the
und favor high humidity as does a pool from
ich water evaporates continously.
Strong air drafts are to be avoided, even
ugh an exchange of air is necessary to avoid
: condensation of water on the glass. Shading
gradually increased from March to May. In
: beginning of fall, remove the shade since the
ht has to be increased for blooming. Repotting
not done at fixed dates, but when the plants
lly need it. This becomes obvious when new
ots with roots develop and reach the edges of
: pot or when there are many shoots on the

rhizome and the old ones are to be eliminated.
Another practice that may be done before
vegetative resumption consists of substituting
some fresh sphagnum on top without repotting
the plants; this has to be done carefully. The
most suitable mixture for *Laelias* (also for *Catt-
leyas* and related types) is made of sphagnum
and osmunda fiber in the ratio of 1:2.

Laelia may be grown together with orchids
having similar demands. In a temperate greenhouse, species and hybrids of *Laelia, Cattleya,
Brassavola* can be grown together, as well as
some *Cymbidium, Coelogyne, Acineta, Houl-
letia,* and in the coldest parts a few *Stanhopea.*

Species and varieties. There are numerous species of *Laelia. L. albida,* from Mexico, with scented flowers that are white with a
pale pink-colored labellum that is striped or yellow in the center.

170

L. anceps, from Mexico, has pink-lilac flowers
which are purple shaded with dark red labellum.

L. crispa, from Brazil, has large flowers that
are pure white or shaded with lilac; the crinkled
labellum is crimson colored and velveted.

L. pumila, native to Brazil, has large and solitary, scented flowers that are rose-purple with a
purple-crimson labellum and a yellow throat.

L. purpurata, from Brazil, is among the largest cultivated orchids has white flowers and a
purple labellum.

164-166. Orchid flowers of *Cattleya* and *Laelio cattleya* are without doubt the most elegant ones for
shapes and colors.

167. A *Cattleya.*

168-169. Imagine what the humid equatorial forests
look like by admiring the peculiar beauty of these
orchids.

170. *Cattleya* growing in the greenhouse.

171

172

173

anda

This is another large and important genus of
Orchidaceae family.

igin. These are old world plants, native
marily to the Himalayas, Burma, China,
lia, the Phillipines, and the South Sea Islands.

orphology. Epiphytic plants, they are
hout pseudobulbs and have an erect and leafy
m; the leaves are distichous, rather fleshy or
hery, plain and sometimes cylindrical. The
vers are large, attached to simple and colored
emes. The sepals are free and spreading and
ilar to the petals; the labellum is trilobous
inserted in the base of the column; on the
er part, it is elongated, forming a sac or ter-

minating in a spur; the lateral lobes are upright
and the median lobe is enlarged and oblong. The
flowers are thick and scented. Their capsules are
oblong with longitudinal ribbings.

Cultivation. The cultivation of *Vanda* is
varied, and is dependent on its particular origin.
Almost all the best varieties need a warm greenhouse and demand high humidity, as well as full
exposure to light. They are grown in a mixture
of sphagnum and osmunda.

Species and varieties. The most important species include the following: *Vanda
Sanderiana,* from the Philippines, has white or
pinkish flowers that have red spots, with a small

yellow labellum leaving red or purple stripes.

V. teres, with white-pinkish colored petals,
yellow lateral lobes with little red dots, and a
purple-pink median lobe.

V. caerulea is a species that may be 3 to 4 feet
tall; its flowers have pale blue petals that are
dark veined and have a dark blue labellum.

V. insignis has light brown petals, spotted on
the inside with dark brown; the labellum has 6
lobes of which the external ones are white and
the median one is purple.

171-173. The architecture of orchid flowers is almost
unchanged in each one of the species that form
this large and selected group of Monocotyledons.

Cymbidium

The species of this genus were among the first to be cultivated because of the abundance and the beauty of the multicolored flowers.

Origins. These are epiphytic, semi-epiphytic, or terrestrial plants, originating from tropical Asiatic regions, from mountain chains in Southern China, from India, from Africa, and from Australia.

Morphology. They have short robust pseudobulbs and a leafy stem. The long floriferous, erect, curved or pendulous scape bears flowers that are shortly peduncled in lateral racemes. The petals are irregular and the labellum has bright colors and is turned downward.

Species and varieties. *Cymbidium insigne* has rose flowers; it has been the chief species of the varieties that are grown for cut flowers.

C. Lowianum has yellow-green colored flowers.

C. grandiflorum is a winter blooming type; its flowers are olive-green.

Cultivation. *Cymbidium* are grown in a cool greenhouse. They are relatively easy to grow. Soil is a mixture of top soil, osmunda fiber, and fir or redwood bark.

174, 176, 177. Flowers of *Paphiopedilum.*
175, 178. Two different forms of flowers of the *Cypripedium* genus.

Cypripedium

The name means "Venus' slipper" and is commonly called Lady Slipper.

Origins. There are about 50 species found in the north temperate zone.

Morphology. They are all terrestrial, herbaceous plants, having a stem that is sometimes reduced. The flower is isolated or in an inflorescence carried by a scape that emerges from the center of the leaves. Characteristic of the flower is the sac-shaped or slipper-shaped labellum. The name *Cypripedium* is erroneously applied to the following species although they are often sold as they are mentioned here. The correct genus is *Paphiopedilum.*

174

176

177

Species and varieties. The following species are commonly grown:

Cypripedium barbatum, native to Southern India and Java, with white and lilac flowers that are rayed with violet and have a dark violet labellum.

C. faireanum, that comes from North Eastern India and has a very large and solitary flower that is light green colored and is scattered with violet on the labellum and on the lateral petals; the back petal is large, white-greenish with longitudinal purple stripes.

C. insigne, native to Nepal, has light green flowers and a reddish labellum; the back petal is edged with white and has a green center and purple spots.

C. delenatii, native to Tonkin, is uniformly pale pink and is scented.

Paphiopedilum

This is a genus of Orchidaceae that is very close to the *Cypripedium* in appearance of the flower; cultural demands of the *Paphiopedilum* are not great.

Origins. They are native to Eastern Asia, the Philippines, Malaysia, and Malacca. They are mostly terrestrial, even though they are sometimes epiphytic.

Morphology. They are stemless plants with a short rhizome, having only a few, sword-like, leathery, uniformly green or spotted leaves. The flowers are large and flashy and are on a scape that starts from the center of the leaves with one or two flowers.

Species and varieties. *Paphiopedilum insigne* is one of the most popular and most cultivated orchids; the flower is green and veined with brown.

P. Rothschildianum, native to New Guinea, is a magnificent flower with a back segment that is yellow and rayed with brown-purple stripes; the inner petals are linear, rigid, and pale green; the lip is dull purple tipped with yellow.

P. paestans, from New Guinea, has yellow petals whose edges display purple warts; it is also rayed in dark red; the yellow labellum is reticulated with brown.

P. Stonei is famous for its beautiful varieties because it has one of the largest blooms.

P. villosum, P. callosum, and *P. Spicerianum,* are other remarkable species.

Cultivation. *Paphiopedilum* can be cultivated in a temperate greenhouse following the rules that we have indicated at the opening of the chapter. The most suitable substratum is a mixture of sphagnum, osmunda fiber, and soil. Varieties are numerous and generally more showy than the species.

179. Geraniums being grown in a hot bed or sheltered frame.

180. Flower bed with *Begonia semperflorens.*

181-182. *Cymbidium* are orchids whose flowers are carried on arching stems.

179

180

181

182

183

185

Greenhouses

The greenhouse, like a house, acquires personality when it is used. It really becomes the expression of the gardener and caretaker. It provides a joy to the owner and a place to relax and reflect.

A greenhouse provides many opportunities to grow plants of all kinds. Plants may be propagated in abundance and each person will develop his own plant interests and collections. There is no end to the challenges that will attract the greenhouse owner. He can grow plants that are native to many parts of the world. By regulating the greenhouse environment and his cultur practices, he may have flowers every day in the year; a changing and challenging line of beaut

183. Interior of a greenhouse: on the benches the are plants of *Coleus, Begonias, Alternanthe.* orchids are in the hanging pots.

184. Greenhouses and hot beds are heated in wint

185. View in a greenhouse.

186. Close up of a hot bed.